P9-EJS-550

ROBERT E. LEE

AND THE RISE OF THE SOUTH

The History of the Civil War

MENDOCINO COUNTY LIBRARY

1000 09 096060 0 4

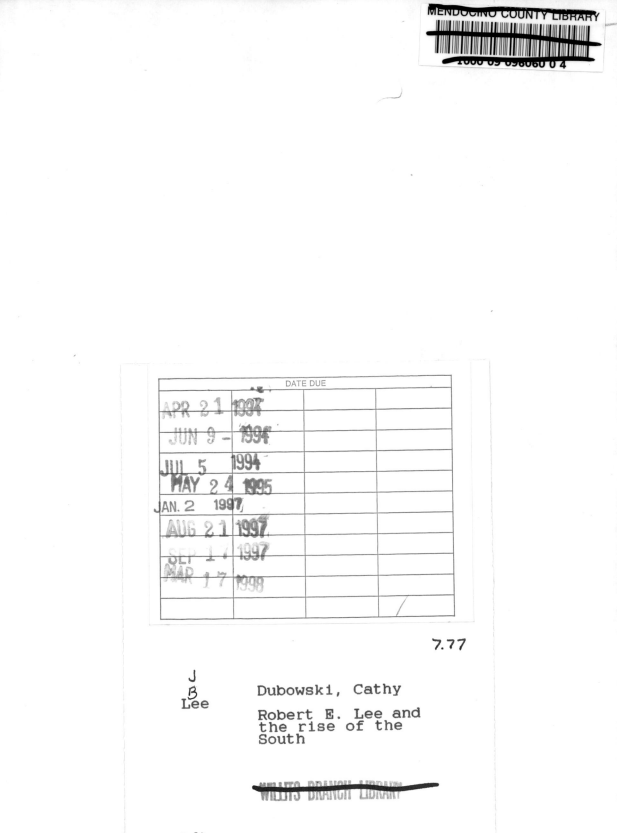

DATE DUE			
APR 21 1994			
JUN 9 - 1994			
JUL 5 1994			
MAY 24 1995			
JAN. 2 1997			
AUG 21 1997			
SEP 1 7 1997			
MAR 1 7 1998			

WILLITS BRANCH LIBRARY

7.77

J
B
Lee

Dubowski, Cathy

Robert E. Lee and
the rise of the
South

GUMDROP BOOKS - Bethany, Missouri

THE HISTORY OF THE CIVIL WAR

ROBERT E. LEE

AND THE RISE OF THE SOUTH

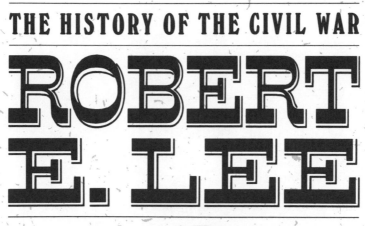

by CATHY EAST DUBOWSKI

INTRODUCTORY ESSAY BY
HENRY STEELE COMMAGER

WILLITS BRANCH LIBRARY

SILVER BURDETT PRESS

Series Editorial Supervisor: Richard G. Gallin
Series Editing: Agincourt Press
Series Consultant: Leah Fortson
Cover and Text Design: Circa 86, Inc.
Maps: Susan Johnston Carlson
Series Supervision of Art and Design: Leslie Bauman

Consultant: Robert M. Goldberg, Department Chairperson, Social
Studies, Oceanside Middle School, Oceanside, New York.

Copyright © 1991 by Cathy East Dubowski
Introduction copyright © 1991 by Henry Steele Commager
Illustrations copyright © 1991 by Alex Bloch

All rights reserved, including the right of reproduction in
whole or in part, in any form. Published by Silver Burdett
Press, Inc., a division of Simon & Schuster, Inc., Prentice Hall
Building, Englewood Cliffs, NJ 07632.

Library of Congress Cataloging-in-Publication Data
Dubowski, Cathy East.
     Robert E. Lee: the rise of the South / by Cathy Dubowski ; with
an introduction by Henry Steele Commager.
         p.   cm. — (The History of the Civil War)
     Includes bibliographical references and index.
     Contents: Recounts the life of the general who commanded the
Southern Army during the Civil War.
     1. Lee, Robert E. (Robert Edward), 1807-1870—Juvenile literature.
2. Generals—United States—Biography—Juvenile literature.
3. Generals—Southern States—Biography—Juvenile literature.
4. Confederate States of America. Army—Biography—Juvenile
literature.   5. United States—History—Civil War, 1861-1865—
Campaigns—Juvenile literature.   [1. Lee, Robert E. (Robert
Edward), 1807-1870.   2. Generals.]   I. Title.   II. Series.
E467.1.L4D82   1991
973.7'3'092—dc20
[B]
[92]   90-39751
ISBN 0-382-24051-0 (pbk.)   ISBN 0-382-09942-7 (lib. bdg.)   CIP
                                                               AC

TABLE OF CONTENTS

Family counts in the South, and nowhere more than in Virginia. This may be because Virginia has produced so many distinguished leaders and warriors: Washington, Jefferson, Madison, Monroe, and Robert E. Lee among them. Lee's father was the famous "Lighthorse" Harry Lee who had fought under Washington, and Lee married the granddaughter of Washington's wife. Lee also had many cousins in his native state. That is doubtless the reason that, when confronted with the toughest decision of his life—whether to stay with the Union or join the South in the Civil War—Lee opted to side with the Confederacy and defend his home state. And perhaps it was also Lee's heritage that led him, at the age of 19, to choose West Point and a military career. That choice would have a profound effect on the course of American history.

Though a loyal Virginian, Lee was also a loyal American. He had fought heroically for his nation in the war with Mexico in the 1840s, and achieved his first military distinction in some of that conflict's bloodiest battles. It was also in that war that Lee had first fought alongside the man he would later call "his right arm" in the Civil War, Thomas "Stonewall" Jackson. Ironically, the man who would later force Lee to surrender the Southern cause, Ulysses S. Grant, had also fought by his side in that war.

It was only when pressed to fight for or against his native state that Lee made the fateful decision to enter into war against the government to which he had sworn a military oath. He would eventually become one of the main factors in that war's disastrous toll. With legendary military brilliance, Lee kept his side in the war despite the Union's enormous advantages in industry and human resources. Using tactics that cost the North dearly, Lee continually led Union armies on long wild goose chases, evading their punches and wearing them out. It was not until Abraham Lincoln put the tough and decisive Ulysses S. Grant in charge that Lee finally met his match in a warrrior spirit every bit as vital as his own.

In the end, the "War Between the States" (as southerners still call it) would be devastating in terms of the numbers of lives taken, the destruction of property, and the cost in natural resources.

Yet, unlike so many wars, the war Lee fought and lost also brought rewards. Slavery was ended; the Constitution was tested and strenghtened. As President Lincoln said in his Gettysburg Address: "... we here highly resolve that these dead shall not have died in vain, that this nation shall have a new birth of freedom."

It was indeed to a new-born nation that Lee returned after his quiet surrender of the Southern forces at Appomattox Court House in 1865. Eventually, the retired commander and beloved hero of the South was offered the presidency of Washington College in Lexington, Virginia. Lee took the post and served there with such distinction that the school changed its name to Washington and Lee University. It was a fitting honor to a man who so loved his heritage and his home.

CIVIL WAR TIME LINE

May 22
Kansas-Nebraska Act states that in new territories the question of slavery will be decided by the citizens. Many Northerners are outraged because this act could lead to the extension of slavery.

1854   **1855**   **1856**   **1857**

May 21
Lawrence, Kansas is sacked by proslavery Missourians.

May 22
Senator Charles Sumner is caned by Preston Brooks for delivering a speech against slavery.

May 24 – 25
Pottawatomie Creek massacre committed by John Brown and four of his sons.

March 6
The Supreme Court, in the *Dred Scott* ruling, declares that blacks are not U. S. citizens, and therefore cannot bring lawsuits. The ruling divides the country on the question of the legal status of blacks.

October 16
Abolitionist John Brown leads a raid on Harpers Ferry, Virginia, causing Southerners to fear further attacks from the North.

January 9 – February 1
Mississippi, Florida, Alabama, Georgia, Louisiana, and Texas secede.
February 4
Seceded states meet to form a new government, the Confederate States of America.
April 13
Fort Sumter, South Carolina, surrenders to Confederacy as Civil War begins.
May 6 – 23
Arkansas, North Carolina, Virginia, and Tennessee secede.
July 21
First Battle of Bull Run/Manassas is won by Confederacy.
July 25
Crittenden Resolution is passed, stating that the purpose of the war is to keep the Union together, not to abolish slavery.
August 6
Confiscation Act is passed, allowing Union to seize property, including slaves, if used in the fight against the Union.
November 6
Jefferson Davis and Alexander Stephens are elected Confederate president and vice president.

1858	1859	1860	1861

November 6
Abraham Lincoln is elected president.
December 20
South Carolina secedes from the Union.

February 6
Fort Henry, Tennessee, is captured.

February 16
Fort Donelson, Tennessee, is captured by Union.

March 9
Monitor and *Merrimack* battle near Hampton Roads, Virginia.

March 23
Shenandoah Valley Campaign opens with Union victory over Maj. Gen. Thomas J. "Stonewall" Jackson.

April 7
Gen. Ulysses S. Grant wins Battle of Shiloh, Tennessee, splitting rebel forces on the Mississippi River.

April 25
New Orleans is captured by Union naval forces led by flag officer David Farragut.

June 19
Slavery is abolished in U. S. territories.

June 25
Gen. Robert E. Lee leads rout of Gen. George McClellan's army in the Seven Days Battles.

July 17
The United States Congress authorizes formation of the first black regiments.

August 29 – 30
Second Battle of Bull Run/Manassas is won by Confederacy.

September 5
Lee leads first Confederate invasion of the North into Maryland.

September 17
Battle of Antietam/Sharpsburg, bloodiest of the war, ends in a stalemate between Lee and McClellan.

1862	1863	1864	1865

January 1
Lincoln issues Emancipation Proclamation, freeing slaves in Confederate states.

March 3
U.S. Congress passes its first military draft.

April 2
Bread riots occur in Richmond, Virginia.

May 1 – 4
Battle of Chancellorsville is won by Confederacy; Stonewall Jackson is accidentally shot by his own troops.

May 22 – July 4
Union wins siege of Vicksburg in Mississippi.

June 3
Lee invades the North from Fredericksburg, Virginia.

July 3
Battle of Gettysburg is won in Pennsylvania by Union.

July 13 – 17
Riots occur in New York City over the draft.

November 19
Lincoln delivers the Gettysburg Address.

March 12
Grant becomes general-in-chief of Union army.
May 5 – 6
Lee and Lt. Gen. James Longstreet defeat Grant at the Wilderness Battle in Virginia.
May 6 – September 2
Atlanta Campaign ends in Union general William Tecumseh Sherman's occupation of Atlanta.
May 8 – 19
Lee and Grant maneuver for position in the Spotsylvania Campaign.
June 3
Grant is repelled at Cold Harbor, Virginia.
June 18, 1864 – April 2, 1865
Grant conducts the Siege of Petersburg, in Virginia, ending with evacuation of the city and Confederate withdrawal from Richmond.
August 5
Admiral Farragut wins Battle of Mobile Bay for Union.
October 6
Union general Philip Sheridan lays waste to Shenandoah Valley, Virginia, cutting off Confederacy's food supplies.
November 8
Lincoln is reelected president.
November 15 – December 13
Sherman's March to the Sea ends with Union occupation of Savannah, Georgia.

March 2
First Reconstruction Act is passed, reorganizing governments of Southern states.

1866   1867   1868   1869

April 9
Civil Rights Act of 1866 is passed. Among other things, it removes states' power to keep former slaves from testifying in court or owning property.

November 3
Ulysses S. Grant is elected president.

January 31
Thirteenth Amendment, freeing slaves, is passed by Congress and sent to states for ratification.
February 1 – April 26
Sherman invades the Carolinas.
February 6
Lee is appointed general-in-chief of Confederate armies.
March 3
Freedman's Bureau is established to assist former slaves.
April 9
Lee surrenders to Grant at Appomattox Courthouse, Virginia.
April 15
Lincoln dies from assassin's bullet; Andrew Johnson becomes president.
May 26
Remaining Confederate troops surrender.

THE GENTLEMAN MUST DECIDE

"I know you will blame me; but you must think
as kindly of me as you can, and believe that I
have endeavored to do what I thought right."
ROBERT E. LEE, TO HIS SISTER, ANNE MARSHALL,
WIFE OF A UNION LOYALIST, APRIL 20, 1861

Mary Lee spent the evening in the family sitting room. Above, her she heard the sound of her husband pacing the floor of their bedroom. More than once she thought she heard him fall to his knees in prayer.

Robert Edward Lee had a decision to make. The most important decision of his career—of his life. He had hoped with all his heart that this moment would never come, that he would not have to choose.

The past 12 months had been stormy ones for the United States. The country was not a hundred years old, and yet the bonds formed among the states in the passion of the American Revolution were unraveling.

Once 13 colonies had joined together to fight a common enemy. Together in battle they had won their independence from the king of England and formed a new nation—the United States of America. Each new state had its own way of life and its own identity, but all the states worked together to create a government unlike any the world had ever known. Here no king or queen handed down orders for all to obey. Here all citizens could have

their say. The people—at least the property-owning white males—
had a voice in how the government should be run.

As the country grew, however, the people who lived in the
North and the people who lived in the South began to grow apart.
Their lives were different in many important ways.

Until the mid-19th century most Americans—in the North and
South—lived on farms. Slaves brought from Africa had been put to
work in many parts of the country, often on tobacco farms. But
things were changing in the North. The small towns and cities
were growing. The development of the steam engine in England
had given the world new ways of making goods such as clothing
and tools. In the United States, the North led the way in this
Industrial Revolution. Factories sprang up throughout New England and the middle Atlantic states, and the mill owners found
plenty of willing hands to work. Each year for several years in a
row, nearly 300,000 European immigrants hoping for a better life
steamed into the country through New York Harbor. Most were
poor and could not speak English well, if at all. Many settled in
cities, crowded into small flats in neighborhoods filled with their
own people. They took whatever work they could find, at any
wages they could get. They helped end the economic need for slave
labor in the North.

But the Industrial Revolution would actually keep the South a
farming region. In 1793, Eli Whitney had invented a machine called
the cotton gin, which could quickly and easily separate the white
fluffy cotton from the seeds. The growing mills in the North and
in Europe were hungry for raw cotton and would buy all they
could get. Cotton grew well in the mild Southern climate, and it
soon passed tobacco, rice, sugar, and indigo as the South's number
one crop. Cotton was King.

Growing and picking cotton was backbreaking work. The only
way to make money from the cotton plantations was by using free
slave labor. Many early Americans had thought slavery would soon
die out. But with the boom in cotton production, the demand for
slaves grew—and the price for slaves rose as well. In the year 1850, a
good strong male slave could cost $1,800—more than most middle-

class people then earned in a year. Of the 10 million people living in the South in that year, more than 3.2 million were now slaves. Most of the white Southerners still lived on small, poor farms, but the wealthy minority who owned plantations and slaves had the strongest voice in politics and government.

More and more, the Northern states and Southern states needed different things from their government. They became like two rival siblings, squabbling over which would get its own way.

The new profits from cotton helped spur the nation's expansion westward, as Southerners looked for new land to develop. New territories and states were created. Though Northern abolitionists believed slavery was wrong and wanted it ended completely, other Northerners were mostly interested in seeing that it did not spread to these new territories. They did not want cheap slave labor to keep white workers out of jobs. People in Southern states believed the federal government should not be able to dictate what a state did within its own borders. They feared the Northern states were becoming a majority in the government, and they wanted to keep the new states "on their side" by keeping slavery legal there.

Abraham Lincoln was elected president on November 6, 1860. He was a member of the new Republican party. He believed in stopping the spread of slavery and allowing it only within the Southern states where it already existed. But Southern states feared such a stand would keep them from expanding cotton production westward and would only lead to meddling within their borders. Days later, on December 20, South Carolina representatives met in Charleston and voted unanimously to secede—completely break away—from the United States of America.

By February 1, 1861, six other states had followed: Mississippi, Florida, Alabama, Georgia, Louisiana, and Texas. That week delegates met in Montgomery, Alabama, to form a new nation, the Confederate States of America. On February 9, they elected Jefferson Davis of Missouri, a former secretary of war, president, and Alexander H. Stephens of Georgia, vice president.

Yet the situation was far from settled. In the speech Lincoln made in taking office, he declared the Union "unbroken." This meant he refused to recognize the right of the Southern states to break away from the United States.

"In your hands, my dissatisfied fellow-countrymen, and not in mine, is the momentous issue of civil war. The government will not assail you. You can have no conflict, without being yourselves the aggressors. You have no oath registered in Heaven to destroy the government, while I shall have the most solemn one to 'preserve, protect and defend' it."

For a while nothing happened. But action was on the horizon. American troops were still stationed at Fort Sumter, on an island in the harbor of Charleston, South Carolina. The Confederates could not have this "foreign" presence on Southern soil, and the new government demanded that the United States leave the fort at once. Lincoln's answer was that he was sending in supplies.

On April 10, Jefferson Davis ordered the fort to be taken if the federal troops still refused to leave. Beginning April 12, General P. G. T. Beauregard fired on the fort for 34 hours. On April 13, the fort's commanding officer, Major Robert Anderson, surrendered and the flag came down. The Union soldiers left for New York, and the Confederates took possession of the fort.

The war had begun. And each president—Lincoln and Davis— realized for certain now that the other man would not yield without a fight.

The next day Lincoln called for 75,000 troops to put down the rebellion. Immediately Virginia, North Carolina, Tennessee, and Arkansas took action to consider secession.

On April 17, the Virginia convention went into a secret session. The next day Lee was called in to Washington for two separate meetings. The first was with Francis P. Blair, Sr., father of Montgomery Blair, Lincoln's postmaster general. Lee later wrote an account of what happened at that meeting:

"I never intimated to any one that I desired the command of the United States Army; nor did I ever have a conversation with but one gentleman, Mr. Francis Preston Blair, on the subject, which was at his invitation, and as I understood, at the instance of President Lincoln. After listening to his remarks, I declined the offer he made me, to take command of the army that was to be

General Winfield Scott, seated, tried to convince Lee to remain with the Union.

brought into the field; stating, as candidly and as courteously as I could, that, though opposed to secession...I could take no part in an invasion of the Southern states."

Lee then met with General Winfield Scott, a fellow Virginian who had been his commanding officer in the Mexican War. Lee told him of his decision. "Lee, you have made the greatest mistake of your life," Scott said. "But I feared it would be so."

The next day Lee read in the *Alexandria Gazette* that the Virginia convention had voted to secede from the Union. The decision would still have to be ratified by the people of Virginia. But their approval was hardly in doubt. Lee realized that all hope for any sort of peaceful settlement was gone.

When he went into the Stabler-Leadbeater Apothecary shop that day to pay a household account, the merchant asked him what he thought of the recent events. Lee replied, "I must say that I am one of those dull creatures that cannot see the good of secession." The merchant copied his words down in the ledger with the note: "Spoken by Colonel R. E. Lee when he paid this bill, April 19, 1861."

So Lee returned to Arlington, to his magnificent home (also called Arlington) to think. From the steps of his home he could see the unfinished dome of the Capitol building. Here he had courted Mary Anne Randolph Custis, his beloved "Mim," the daughter of George Washington's adopted son. The house was filled with objects tying them to the Founding Father: a painting of Martha

Washington, family heirlooms, George Washington's camp furniture and letters.

His own family had strong ties to Virginia and the founding of the nation. Lee was the son of Henry Lee, a cavalry hero of the Revolution. Two Lees had signed the Declaration of Independence.

He was a Virginian and an American. Now he would have to choose between the two.

What made his decision even harder was that he was an honor graduate of West Point and had spent 32 years in service to the United States Army. He had fought under General Winfield Scott and earned his respect in the Mexican War.

He was against secession: "Secession is nothing but revolution," he once wrote.

He was against slavery: "There are few, I believe in this enlightened age, who will not acknowledge that slavery as an institution is a moral and political evil....I think it a greater evil to the white than to the black race."

After supper that night, he asked to be alone. He went upstairs to think through his decision. He had to have an answer by morning.

Sometime after midnight, he came downstairs. "Well, Mary," he said. "The question is settled." He showed her the two letters he had written.

> Arlington, Virginia (Washington City P.O.)
> 20 April 1861

Hon. Simon Cameron
Secty of War

Sir:

I have the honor to tender [offer] the resignation of my commission [military rank and power] as Colonel of the 1st Regt. of Cavalry.

> Very resp'y Your Obedient Servant,
> R. E. Lee
> Col 1st Cav'y
> Arlington, Virginia
> April 20, 1861

The second letter was to his friend and former commanding officer, General Winfield Scott:

General:

Since my interview with you on the 18th inst. I have felt that I ought no longer to retain my commission in the Army. I therefore tender my resignation, which I request you will recommend for acceptance. It would have been presented at once but for the struggle it has cost me to separate myself from a service to which I have devoted the best years of my life, and all the ability I possessed.

During the whole of that time—more than a quarter of a century—I have experienced nothing but kindness from my superiors and a most cordial friendship from my comrades. To no one, General, have I been as much indebted as to yourself for uniform kindness and consideration, and it has always been my ardent desire to merit your approbation [approval]. I shall carry to the grave the most grateful recollections of your kind consideration, and your name and fame shall always be dear to me.

Save in defense of my native State, I never desire again to draw my sword.

Be pleased to accept my most earnest wishes for the continuance of your happiness and prosperity, and believe me most truly yours,

R. E. Lee

After months of indecision, the town of Alexandria, Virginia, filled with the sounds of jubilation that echoed across the South. For now, war was the future, war was action. No blood had been spilled; no colorful cotton dresses yet changed for widow's black. War was still a beautiful and glorious cause to celebrate, a symbol of state pride and independence.

But not at Lee's Arlington. A neighbor said, "The house was as if there had been a death in it, for the army was to him home and country."

Lee wrote to his brother that day that "I had wished to wait till the Ordinance of Secession should be acted on by the people of Virginia; but war seems to have commenced, and I am liable at any time to be ordered to duty which I could not conscientiously perform.... I had to act at once. I am now a private citizen, and have no other ambition than to remain at home...."

And while all around him people came together in celebration, Lee seemed to be among the few who were already thinking of the separation the war would bring.

His sister, Anne Marshall, lived in Baltimore, Maryland, and was the wife of a Union loyalist. Lee tried to explain to her his pain in choosing a course that would put them on opposite sides of the gun.

My Dear Sister:

I am grieved at my inability to see you.... I have been waiting for a 'more convenient season,' which has brought to many before me deep and lasting regret. Now we are in a state of war which will yield to nothing. The whole South is in a state of revolution, into which Virginia, after a long struggle, has been drawn; and though I recognise no necessity for this state of things.... yet in my own person I had to meet the question whether I should take part against my native State.

With all my devotion to the Union and the feeling of loyalty and duty of an American citizen, I have not been able to make up my mind to raise my hand against my relatives, my children, my home. I have therefore resigned my commission in the Army, and save in defense of my native State, with the sincere hope that my poor services may never be needed, I hope I may never be called upon to draw my sword....

A Loyal Son

"How can I live without Robert? He is both son and daughter to me."

ANN CARTER LEE, SPEAKING OF HER SON'S DEPARTURE FOR WEST POINT

Robert Edward Lee was only three years old the day the carriage pulled away forever from his first home, Stratford Hall. The magnificent Southern plantation overlooking the Potomac River had taken more than five years to build in the 1720s, and it was made of the finest materials found anywhere in Virginia and England. It had been the pride of the Lees of Virginia for more than two generations.

Robert's father, Henry Lee, was well known as "Light-Horse Harry" because of his dashing service as Chief of Cavalry during the American Revolution. He had moved into the grand Stratford Hall in 1782, when he married his wealthy cousin, Matilda Lee, who had inherited Stratford from her brother. It was a happy marriage. In five years they had four children, but only a boy and a girl—Lucy Grymes Lee and Henry Lee IV (called Henry Lee Junior)—survived the illnesses of childhood. When Matilda died in 1790, she left Stratford Hall in trust for their children. Henry, Sr., could stay on, but only until their son, Henry, Jr., came of age and took over the mansion himself.

Highlights in the Life of Robert E. Lee

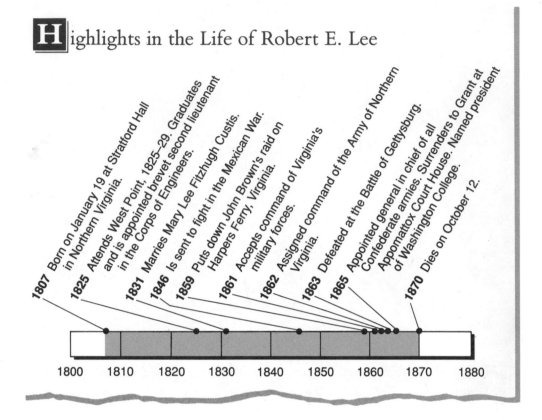

Three years later, the 37-year-old widower fell in love again, this time with a 20-year-old woman named Ann Hill Carter. She was also from one of Virginia's finest and wealthiest families. Her father, Charles Carter, was known as "King Carter," and they lived on the elegant Shirley plantation on the James River.

Harry, always the eager soldier, had been planning to dash off to Paris to fight in the French Revolution. King Carter would not hear of his daughter marrying someone so foolish and reckless— even if he was a Lee! So Harry agreed to stay, and he and Ann were married. At the time, Harry was governor of Virginia, and they spent the first two years of their marriage in Richmond. When the term ended, Harry moved his older children, his new wife, and their first child—Algernon Sidney Lee—to Stratford Hall. Soon after, their infant son died.

Still, the marriage started out happy, and Harry Lee seemed to have everything going for him. He was a hero of the American Revolution. He served three one-year terms as governor of Virginia in the 1790s. While a member of Congress in 1799, he delivered the oration at the funeral of his close friend George Washington, and his words honoring the first president would always be remembered: "...first in war, first in peace, and first in the hearts of his countrymen." Harry had even been named as a possible successor to Washington as president.

But somewhere Harry's good fortune had begun to change. He loved adventure—perhaps that was what made him such a dashing war hero. Now he became adventurous in his business dealings, speculating in wild schemes that he dreamed would bring him great fortunes. But in these adventures he always seemed to suffer staggering defeats. He loaned a friend $40,000, a huge amount of money at that time, to invest in a land deal—but the friend died, and the money was never repaid. Other get-rich-quick schemes followed. The more money he lost, the more reckless his risk-taking became.

Soon Stratford's huge staff of servants and slaves was gone, and so was much of the cherished furniture. Piece by piece, Harry's land holdings were sold off to settle accounts. A few loyal friends still came to call despite his increasingly bad reputation, but by far the family's most frequent visitors were former lenders looking for money. Even his wife Ann could not help him. King Carter, who had never trusted Harry, had locked up Ann's inheritance in a trust, from which she received only a small income.

Ann had given birth to three more children during this time: Charles Carter Lee (1798), Anne Kinlock Lee (1800), and Sydney Smith Lee (1802). Harry was often away from Stratford on some new business scheme, leaving his wife to look after the children and bolt the doors against bill collectors. It must have been a humiliating experience for a woman born into wealth and status. But Ann Carter Lee rarely complained. In the summer of 1806, Ann, once again expecting, decided to go to Shirley to visit her father. She gathered her children into the family's carriage, which was so run-down they would not be able to use it on their trip home. When the family at last got to Shirley, they found the huge mansion in mourning. Her father had died. Grief-stricken, Ann stayed there until December, then took her children home through the cold winter weather in a cheap open carriage. Ann came down with a terrible cold that stayed with her as she faced the birth of her fifth child.

Into this sad state of aristocratic poverty, Robert Edward Lee was born on January 19, 1807. Ann named her son after her two brothers. He was born in the same front corner bedroom at Stratford Hall as Richard Henry Lee and Francis Lightfoot Lee, two signers of the Declaration of Independence.

Growing up, Robert rarely saw his father. Harry spent more time than ever away on business, chasing ever-elusive riches. Soon he had lost everything he owned. In 1809, he was sent to jail because he could not pay his debts. While in prison, he started writing a book about his experiences during the Revolution. Perhaps that would earn the family some money.

Then came the inevitable. Henry Lee IV, heir to Stratford Hall, came of age. Ann waited until Harry got out of jail in 1810. Late that year, the family bundled their modest belongings into their last rickety carriage and moved to the nearby town of Alexandria. The family settled into a small brick house on Cameron Street. That winter a sixth child, Catherine Mildred, was born. Then Harry sold his book, and immediately planned to write others. Perhaps here the family would have a second chance at happiness.

But trouble seemed to hunt for Harry Lee. In June 1812, when Robert was five and a half, the United States went to war with England once again. Harry was against the war. He sympathized with his friend Alexander C. Hanson, anti-war editor of the *Baltimore Federal Republican*, whose offices had been attacked and destroyed by an angry pro-war mob. While Harry was visiting Hanson at his temporary offices in July, another mob attacked. The soldier in Harry took charge of the defense. Shots were fired; a man in the street was killed. The militia arrived and took Harry, Hanson, and his supporters to the safest place possible—the city jail. But after midnight, the drunken mob broke into the jail. A few of the "prisoners" escaped, but the others were beaten nearly to death with clubs. The attackers stuck penknives into Harry's body and poured hot candle wax in his eyes to see if he was still alive. One man even tried to cut off his nose, leaving him disfigured for life. Doctors managed to save his life that night, but he would be a crippled invalid for the rest of his life. In the early summer of 1813, with the help of President James Monroe, he went to Barbados, an island in the West Indies. He hoped the warmer climate would improve his health.

The family sadly said good-bye to him, for despite his failures, they still loved their dashing Light-Horse Harry. Sometimes he would write letters home, in which he rambled on about fame and virtue. In one letter to his son Charles Carter, Harry Lee wrote: "Robert, who was always good, will be confirmed in his happy turn of mind by his ever watchful and affectionate mother."

Robert and his family would never see Light-Horse Harry again.

Ann Lee, raised in wealth, was left to raise and educate five children alone and with very little money. She was frail in health, but strong in spirit. She taught her children to be prudent, to accept their situation without complaint, and most of all, to be careful with money. Though they were poor in material things, they were rich in family and friends. Alexandria was overflowing with relatives from both sides of the family, and Robert had dozens of Lee and Carter cousins to play with. They swam and fished in the Potomac River.

Ann often took her children to visit Shirley Plantation, which was always filled with Carter cousins and laughter and love. There were so many Carters, in fact, that the family had its own schools, one for girls and one for boys. It was among these fun-loving, affectionate Carters that Robert received his first formal education.

To save money, the family moved into a smaller home on Washington Street. Then in February 1818, they received a letter from Harry Lee: he was coming home! But soon after boarding a ship for the States, Harry became ill again, and he was put ashore at

Cumberland Island, Georgia. He stayed with the son of General Nathanael Greene, his commander during the war.

Light-Horse Harry would never reach home, would never see his family again. On March 25, 1818, he died. He was given a full military funeral and buried on the island.

Soon afterward, Robert's older brother, Charles Carter Lee, graduated from Harvard and began practicing law in Washington. His brother Sydney Smith Lee was appointed a midshipman in the navy.

Robert, at age 11, became the man of the house. His mother was becoming an invalid and needed a great deal of attention and care. His older sister, Anne, was ill with a nervous disorder. Sister Catherine was still a child. Robert looked after them all with a patient, affectionate devotion that would become a fundamental aspect of his character throughout his life. He did much of the housework and marketing, and took care of the horses. He was

tender and attentive with his mother, and he told her jokes and funny stories to amuse her.

A relative arranged for the smaller family to move into a much more comfortable home on Orinoco Street. When Robert was 13, he started school at the Alexandria Academy, where he studied Latin and Greek and discovered that he was very good at math. By the time he was 16, he had finished his courses and was thinking of his future. It appears that he considered only one profession: soldier.

Robert had grown up hearing the legends of his father's glorious adventures during the Revolutionary War. He had watched proudly as his brother Sydney Smith Lee went off to join the navy. The town of Alexandria was filled with monuments to the war's heroes, and with memories of George Washington, who had been a friend to Robert's father. Washington had worshiped at Christ Church, near Cameron Street, and had met to talk of revolution at Gadsby's Tavern. Just a short way down the river was Washington's beautiful white mansion, Mount Vernon.

The Revolution had ended only 30 years earlier. Joining the military was an honorable and prestigious career choice for a young man of the 1820s. Robert decided his best course of action was to apply to the United States Military Academy at West Point.

For an aristocrat with no fortune, it was an honorable way to acquire a top education at no cost. To attend, a boy had to meet certain requirements. He had to be between the ages of 14 and 20, stand at least four feet nine inches tall, and be in good health. He had to have fair knowledge of reading, writing, and arithmetic. As payment for his education, he had to agree to stay in the army for at least five years, plus the four years at school. The requirements were well within Robert's reach, but competition for the few positions was tough. Candidates for West Point were named by the secretary of war, and then appointed by the president of the United States. One of Robert's distant relatives, William H. Fitzhugh, whose home Ravensworth was nearby, agreed to help him. Fitzhugh personally submitted Robert's letter of application to John C. Calhoun, secretary of war.

On March 11, 1824, Robert learned he had been appointed to West Point. However, the waiting list was so long that he could not actually be admitted to school until July 1, 1825—a full year away.

Robert was disappointed, but it was an exciting year despite the delay. In October, the Marquis de Lafayette visited Alexandria. The famous French nobleman had fought as a general on the American side in the Revolutionary War, and had become friendly with Harry Lee. On October 14, 1824, he made a special visit to the family of his deceased friend.

Robert continued his studies at a new school run by Benjamin Hallowell, a Quaker. He remembered Robert as gentlemanly, respectful, and a model student whose work was always done neatly and on time.

At last, in June 1825, Robert took first a steamer and then a stagecoach to reach West Point. Leaving home for the first time must have been exciting, but it could not have been easy. His mother remarked soon after: "How can I live without Robert? He is both son and daughter to me."

When Robert E. Lee first saw West Point, it was a fairly new school, not yet 25 years old. A few drab buildings looked out over a large parade ground with a view of the Hudson River. It was a small school with lots of rules: Cadets could not drink, smoke, play cards, or have games, novels, or cooking utensils in their rooms. They could not form clubs or societies without approval. There were strict limits on visitors, hours spent reading, and places where cadets could go. Cadets earned demerits when they broke the rules—and many earned plenty, for the young school had quite a few discipline problems with its rowdy young men.

One of Robert's classmates, Jefferson Davis, was often in trouble. He was the man who would one day lead the Confederate government as president. Davis was court-martialed for drinking in a forbidden tavern. One night he nearly killed himself falling down a cliff in the dark, trying to avoid being caught in an area that was off-limits. Another time there was a big scandal over an eggnog party; several cadets were dismissed from school, and

Davis was confined to quarters. One report from the superinten- dent—the head of West Point—described the cadets' habit of drinking with their backs turned to each other. That way, when the cadets were questioned, they could truthfully say they had seen no one drinking.

Robert's page in the *Record of Delinquencies* was filled with demerits—only none of them were his. Another cadet's page was so filled with reports of his wrongdoings that the clerk had to use Robert's blank to list them all. Lee, in fact, was the first cadet not to earn a single demerit in his entire four years at West Point.

But Robert was not a stick-in-the-mud. He was an excellent student, and he was not only well liked but admired by teachers and fellow students alike. Handsome and gentlemanly, he seemed made to wear a uniform. Friends called him the "Marble Model," and one said years later, "His personal appearance surpassed in manly beauty that of any cadet in the corps. Though firm in his position and perfectly erect, he had none of the stiffness so often assumed by men who affect to be very strict in their ideas of what is military."

In Robert's first year he ranked third in his class. From then on, he consistently held on to the number-two spot. He was excellent at mathematics, and in his second year he won a position as acting professor, which paid the goodly sum of $10 a month.

His outstanding work also won him a furlough—a leave of absence. Cadets were not allowed to go home or leave school for any reason—except for illness or a death in the family—until they had been at West Point for two years. Even then they needed the approval of the superintendent and permission from home. In 1827, at the end of his second year, Robert did well on his exams and again placed second in his class. With permission to leave, he went to visit his mother, who now lived in Georgetown. She was 54 and in failing health, but together they spent much of Robert's time off visiting Carter relatives.

It is also likely that he spent some time with 20-year-old Mary Anne Randolph Custis, whom he had known since they were children. Her father, George Washington Parke Custis, was the adopted son of George Washington, who had raised him and his sister Eleanor at Mount Vernon. Lee would see more of Mary in the future.

When his leave was over, Robert returned to West Point and threw himself into his work. He took even harder courses: chemistry, technical drawing, and physics. Along with the other cadets, he also learned the practical lessons of war: how to make and read maps, how to build forts and bridges, how to march for hours on end, and how to handle guns and cannon.

Robert had begun West Point in a class of 105. When he graduated in June 1829, he was one of only 46. Robert had had an outstanding four years. His reputation among teachers and fellow cadets was spotless. He had among the highest marks for military tactics and artillery, engineering, and conduct, and ranked number two overall in the final class standing. Top students were allowed to choose what field of the army they wanted, and Lee chose the engineer corps. Upon graduation he was appointed brevet second lieutenant in the Corps of Engineers.

Robert was 22 and had grown to his full height of 5 feet 10 ½ inches tall. He was quite handsome, with deep brown eyes, thick dark hair, and perfect manners. There was already a dignity about him that would earn him respect throughout his life, and a gentle sense of humor that would always win him friends. He had done well to save $103.58 from his cadet pay, and he had two months' furlough. The mysteries of his future lay before him. He went home to await word of his assignment.

But the summer after his graduation was to be one of the saddest of his life. His mother had gone to stay with the Fitzhughs at Ravensworth, and she was dying. Though only 56, she had struggled to raise her 5 children alone and had simply worn herself out. Once again, Robert became her faithful nurse and rarely left her side. He gave her her medicines and tried to get her to eat. Perhaps he read to her or tried to amuse her with stories of the pranks played by the West Point cadets. Nothing could be done for her, and on July 10, Robert sat with Ann Hill Carter Lee and watched her die. She had been both mother and father to Robert, and he grieved quietly for her as he went to Georgetown to settle her estate.

In August, he returned to Virginia to visit relatives while waiting to receive his military orders. Often he galloped up into the hills overlooking Alexandria, to Arlington, the magnificent home of George Washington Parke Custis. He came to see the man's only daughter, Mary Anne Randolph Custis, who was distantly related to him through her mother, Mary Lee Fitzhugh Custis. Mary was 21 now, a pale, fragile young woman with a quick smile. They had known each other as children, and now their friendship had grown into love. Before anything could be decided, however, the army interrupted their courtship.

On August 11, 1829, Robert received his orders. By November he was to report to Cockspur Island, at the mouth of the Savannah River in South Carolina.

His life as a soldier had begun.

A FATHER AND AN ENGINEER

"Everybody and everything—his family, his
friends, his horse, his dog—loves Colonel Lee."
A BALTIMORE WOMAN, OVERHEARD
BY LEE'S SON, ROBERT, JR.

or a young man in love, fresh out of West Point, Cockspur
Island, South Carolina, must have been a dreadful first
assignment. But Robert E. Lee's experience here would
serve him well in the future.

The War of 1812 with Great Britain had made clear how
vulnerable American ports were to naval attack. Lee was going to
help construct Fort Pulaski, part of a large defense system of stone
forts being built at major ports along the East Coast. Major Samuel
Babcock was the man in charge, but he was too sickly to work on-
site, so Lee managed most of the project. He was young and
inexperienced for such an assignment, but then Lee had often
shouldered responsibility beyond his age.

Occasionally Lee got away from his work to visit friends in
nearby Savannah, and the handsome young officer was quite
popular with the ladies. But Lee spent most of his time at the
swampy island up to his armpits in mud and water, fighting
mosquitoes—and enduring scandal. His half-brother, Henry Lee
IV, was up for a government appointment, and the congressional
investigation dug up damaging facts about him. Henry's wife

Anne had become addicted to morphine after the death of their two-year-old daughter. Henry then had an affair with her younger sister Elizabeth. On top of this scandal, there were financial problems, and Henry had had to sell Stratford Hall to pay his debts. Never again would this grand ancestral home belong to a Lee.

Robert had always been on good terms with his half-brother, but news of such conduct, and the further disgrace of his father's name, was humiliating for a young man with such a high sense of integrity. Only occasional visits to see Mary Custis made the days easier to endure.

In May 1831, Lee was transferred to Old Point Comfort, Virginia, to work at Fort Monroe. Lee was delighted with the move because he was much closer to Arlington. As soon as possible, he traveled up the Potomac by boat to visit Mary. He had some unfinished business to attend to. One day during the visit he sat in the grand hall of Arlington reading aloud to Mary and her mother, Mary Lee Fitzhugh Custis—a novel by the Scottish writer Sir Walter Scott, which was too exciting to put down. After several chapters, Mrs. Custis interrupted the young man. Mr. Lee looked awfully tired, she said. Then she told Mary to go into the dining room to get him something to eat. As soon as Mary left the room, Lee excused himself and followed her. There at the sideboard, as Mary bent over to cut a slice of fruitcake, Lee asked her to marry him. The answer was a quick yes.

Mr. George Washington Custis, however, had strong doubts about the marriage. Of the Custises' four children, all had died in infancy except their precious Mary. He would not have chosen for her a young man with a ruined family fortune and only a soldier's pay to live on. But he had nothing against Lee himself, and Mary was of age to marry without his permission. At last he gave them his blessing.

The huge formal wedding took place at Arlington on June 30, 1831, a day so rainy the minister arrived soaked to the skin. A month later the young couple settled down at Fort Monroe. Mary insisted that they would live happily on Lee's salary—without any financial help from her father.

MRS. ROBERT E. LEE

Mary Custis, who had known Robert E. Lee from childhood, became his wife of 14 years.

Mr. and Mrs. Lee adored each other, but they were different in many ways. He was never late; she was never on time. He was orderly and neat; she was often careless about how she dressed and kept house. He was always tactful; she always spoke her mind. Yet theirs would prove to be a long and happy marriage, and they would have 7 children in 14 years. The many letters they wrote to each other throughout their lives were filled with affection and showed a never-ending respect and devotion.

Soon after the Lees arrived at Fort Monroe, a bloody slave uprising in Southampton County, less than 50 miles away, shocked the South. On August 22, a black preacher named Nat Turner and a handful of other slaves killed their master's family with axes. As they ran, they rounded up arms and other slaves and killed more than 50 white men, women, and children. Soon the area was swarming with troops, including many from Fort Monroe. Lee was a staff officer and was kept behind, but he was greatly troubled by the event. Many blacks—innocent and guilty—were killed by the soldiers. Turner and several others were captured, sentenced, and hanged.

The uprising struck fear throughout the South. New troops were assigned to Fort Monroe, so that now more than 680 men were stationed there. Among them was a classmate of Lee's from West Point, a fellow Virginian named Joseph E. Johnston. Lee was delighted to renew their friendship.

Soon things quieted down again at Fort Monroe. An only child, Mary often returned to Arlington to visit her parents, and Lee joined her whenever he could.

The Lees' first child was born September 16, 1832, and they named him George Washington Custis Lee, after Mary's father. Lee was delighted with the baby. Mary wrote, "If he wakes up in the night and cries and Robert speaks to him, he stops immediately..."

In 1834, Lee was given a post as assistant to the Chief of Engineers in the War Department in Washington, D.C. Mary was thrilled, and in November the new family moved into Arlington. It was only to be until they could find their own home, but they wound up staying there four years. Lee grew quite fond of warm-hearted Mrs. Custis, and even Mr. Custis got over his opposition to his daughter's marriage. The beautiful white mansion had plenty of room, and it was filled with the belongings of Lee's hero, George Washington. Lee had been an aristocrat without land or money. Now, through his wife, he was part heir to Arlington, and he would grow to cherish it almost as much as he did the memory of his family's lost Stratford Hall. From the eight-column portico, Lee could look across the grounds and the Potomac River to the city of Washington.

Every workday morning, Lee would rise early and ride into Washington to his job at the War Department. Here Lee would become highly qualified in his field of engineering. But much of the heavy workload was boring, and he did not feel quite comfortable in an office that was often filled with petty jealousies and bickering. Each night, however, he escaped to the graceful Arlington and his delightful wife and son. Often the home was

filled with interesting guests and festive parties. These were among
the happiest years in Lee's life.

In the spring of 1835, Lee was given a pleasant break when he
was sent to the Great Lakes region to do some surveying. When he
returned in October, however, he was alarmed to find that his dear
Mary was gravely ill following the birth of their second child,
Mary Custis. She was not able to walk until early the next year.
That summer he took his wife for treatment at the mineral springs
in the Virginia mountains. Gradually her health improved, but she
was left partially lame. Lee was brokenhearted to see his bright-
eyed, delicate Mary suffer such pain. A relative recalled: "I never
saw a man so changed and saddened." Then, as Mrs. Lee got
better, the children got whooping cough, and when they got better,
Mrs. Lee came down with mumps. It was a difficult year, as filled
with worry as the year before had been filled with joy.

Lee's promotion to first lieutenant on September 21 was a
welcome boost. Yet he was becoming more depressed about his job
among the squabbling bureaucrats, and he even considered resigning. His only refuge was in his family. Then, in 1837, an
opportunity came to get out of the office in Washington and work
on a project in St. Louis, Missouri. In May of that year, Mary had
another son, and they named him after William Henry Fitzhugh of
Ravensworth, Mary's uncle and the man who had nominated Lee
for West Point. As soon as Lee was assured that both Mary and
little "Rooney," as he was called, were out of danger, he left for St.
Louis.

St. Louis, however, turned out to be "the dearest [most expen-
sive] and dirtiest place I was ever in," he wrote. "Our daily
expenses about equal our daily pay." In his letters home to Mary at
Arlington, he sounded lonely and homesick. He had grown up in a
family where the father had often been away, and he did not like
leaving Mary to look after their children alone: "Oh, what pleasure
I lose in being separated from my children. Nothing can compensate me for that; still I must remain here, ready to perform what
little service I can, and hope for the best."

Lee's assignment was a difficult and expensive one. For the first time he would be in charge, and he designed the project himself. The Mississippi River was depositing a sandbar near St. Louis and threatening to block this busy river port. Lee recommended building two huge dikes that would redirect the river and dissolve the sandbar. He had to deal with angry landowners and politicians and funding problems. But he worked tirelessly at the project for two and a half years.

The mayor of the city wrote of Lee: "He went in person with the hands [workers] every morning about sunrise and worked day by day in the hot broiling sun.... He shared the hard task and common fare and rations furnished to the common laborers, eating at the same table... He maintained and preserved under all circumstances his dignity and gentlemanly bearing, winning and commanding the esteem, regard, and respect of every one under him."

Although the project would run out of government money before it could be finished, Lee's work earned him a reputation as an excellent, dependable engineer. On August 7, 1838, he was promoted to captain. But his small pay increase hardly kept up

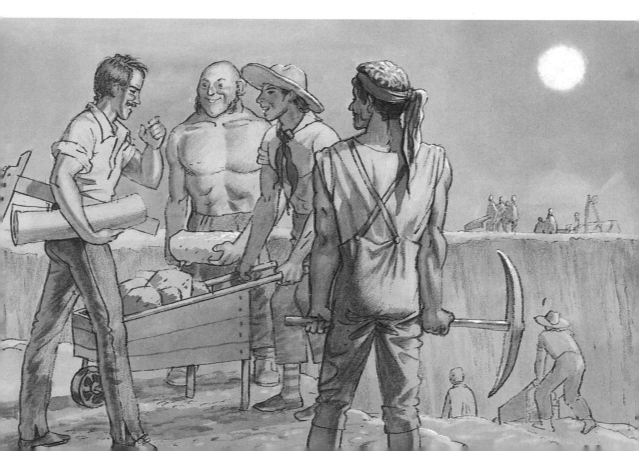

with his growing family. The next June, his second daughter, Annie Carter Lee, was born.

Following the St. Louis project, Lee spent the next few years inspecting several forts along the East Coast (forts that would eventually become important defenses in the Civil War). The winter of 1840–41 was spent in North Carolina. In the spring he went to New York City to work on four forts guarding New York Harbor. This time he took his family, including new baby Eleanor Agnes. They made their home at Fort Hamilton, though they often spent long holidays at Arlington. Two more children were born while they were there: Robert E. Lee, Jr., in October 1843, and Mildred Childe Lee, in February 1846.

Over the years Lee was often separated from his family because of his career, but he was always a loving father, and his children adored and respected him. Years later Robert, Jr., wrote: "I always knew that it was impossible to disobey my father. I felt it in me, I never thought why, but was perfectly sure when he gave an order that it had to be obeyed. I could sometimes [get around], and at times took liberties with her orders...but exact obedience to...my father was a part of my life and being..."

This discipline was born out of Lee's love for his children. He once wrote to Mary: "You do not know how much I have missed you and the children, my dear Mary. To be alone in a crowd is very solitary....I hope you are all well and will continue so, and, therefore, must again urge you to be very prudent and careful of those dear children. If I could only get a squeeze at that little fellow, turning up his sweet mouth to 'keese baba!' You must not let him run wild in my absence, and will have to exercise firm authority over all of them. This will not require severity or even strictness, but constant attention and an unwavering course. Mildness and forbearance will strengthen their affection for you, while it will maintain your control over them."

One of Lee's greatest pleasures was to pile into the bed with all the children and tell them stories while they tickled his hands and feet. Robert, Jr., recalled: "He would often tell us the most delightful stories, and then there was no nodding. Sometimes, however, our interest in his wonderful tales became so engrossing that we would forget to do our duty—when he would declare, 'No tickling, no story!'"

One day while supervising work on the forts by boat, Lee rescued a stray dog from the water. He named the terrier Dart and took her home to the family. When Dart had puppies, Lee was especially fond of a little black and tan one that he named Spec. According to Robert, Jr., "My father would not allow his tail and ears to be cropped. When he grew up, he accompanied us everywhere and was in the habit of going to church with the family." One day, however, Lee decided the dog distracted the children too much from the sermon. So Spec was left upstairs while the family went to church. Minutes later, Spec jumped out of the second-story window and ran to the church just as the family was going inside. Then he "went in with them as usual, much to the joy of the children. After that he was allowed to go to church whenever he wished. My father was very fond of him, and loved to talk to him and about him as if he were really one of us." Indeed, Lee's letters were often filled with news about Spec. Once, when Mary and the children were visiting Arlington, he wrote: "I am very solitary, and my only company is my dog and cats. But 'Spec' has become so jealous now that he will hardly let me look at the cats. . . . I catch him sometimes sitting up looking at me so intently that I am for a moment startled."

Years later a Baltimore woman visiting the Lees remarked, "Everybody and everything—his family, his friends, his horse, and his dog—loves Colonel Lee."

The five years spent in New York were a happy time for the large Lee family. In peacetime, life for a soldier and his family was not so different from that of a civilian family. Lee had a respected position in the army and had learned a great deal about constructing coastal defenses. But at age 39, he was a soldier who had never faced battle.

Then on May 13, 1846, the United States declared war on Mexico. Lee's lessons of war were about to begin.

A Soldier

"You have no idea what a horrible sight a field of
battle is."

Lee writing to his brother Custis after his
first taste of battle at Cerro Gordo, Mexico

The United States had grown beyond all imagination since
the days of Washington and Light-Horse Harry Lee. The
country was expanding westward with an endless appetite
for land. In the Southwest, conflicts with Mexico arose over
boundaries. When the United States annexed Texas in 1845, the
conflict grew into war.

Many Americans had come to believe in what one journalist
called "Manifest Destiny"—that the United States had the God-
given right to expand across North America to the Pacific Ocean.
Not everyone accepted this idea or supported the war. Many people
believed it was an out-and-out land grab, and that President James
K. Polk had started the war for just that purpose. Some people
believed it was a plot to expand slavery into more new territory.
One young congressman named Abraham Lincoln nearly ruined
his career when he charged that the war was "immoral and
unnecessary." Writer-philosopher Henry David Thoreau went to
jail rather than pay taxes that would help pay for the war. A young
lieutenant named Ulysses S. Grant believed the army had been
"sent to provoke a fight."

Lee, however, was a career soldier and was never one to get involved in heated arguments about politics. He simply waited to hear what his orders would be.

While he waited, General Zachary Taylor led American troops into battle with the Mexicans at Palo Alto (May 8) and Resaca de la Palma (May 9). That summer, General S. W. Kearny was marching toward Sante Fe and Taylor was going after Monterrey with the hopes of finding Mexican general and dictator Antonio López de Santa Anna.

On August 19, 1846, Lee received orders to report to Washington. From there he would report to Brigadier General John E. Wool in San Antonio, Texas, to fight in the war. While in Washington, the ever-orderly Lee filed his only known will before leaving for the scene of battle. He left everything to Mary, "in full confidence that she will use it to the best advantage in the education and care of my children."

Robert E. Lee during the Mexican War.

WILLITS BRANCH LIBRARY

When Lee arrived in San Antonio, his first duties were as an engineer, building roads and bridges for the army to travel on. Mary and the children stayed at Arlington, and the Lees spent their first Christmas apart. He wrote to Mary: "We have had many happy Christmases together. It is the first time we have been entirely separated at this holy time since our marriage. I hope it does not interfere with your happiness, surrounded as you are by father, mother, children, and dear friends. I therefore trust you are well and happy, and that this is the last time I shall be absent from you during my life...."

On Christmas morning, word came that the enemy was about to attack the U.S. camp, but the Mexicans never arrived. Lee volunteered to go on a scouting mission to find their army. By accident he did not meet up with his cavalry escort, but he could not turn back. He rode on into enemy territory in darkness with only his Mexican guide. Soon he found the tracks of mules and wagons, but no sign of artillery. He rode on and saw in the distance what looked like campfires. Another soldier might have been satisfied that the enemy had been found. Lee's Mexican guide begged him to turn back or they would be caught. But Lee was not satisfied. Soon he came to a stream. On the other side, he saw what looked like hundreds of white tents pitched on the hillside. Still he pressed on. At last, in the moonlight, he saw the "enemy" for what it was—a large flock of snowy white sheep tended by a few Mexican drovers. Lee knew a little Spanish, and he questioned the men. He learned that Santa Anna's troops had not yet crossed the mountains.

Lee galloped back to camp to deliver the news. He had ridden 40 miles by horseback that night. After only three hours' rest, he led a cavalry expedition beyond where he had been the night before, and they were successful in locating the enemy. Lee was transferred before a battle could be fought, but his work provided General Taylor with the information he needed to defeat Santa Anna's troops at Buena Vista on February 22 and 23, 1847.

In a letter home, Lee sent a message to Spec: "Tell him I wish he was here with me. He would have been of great service in telling

Ulysses S. Grant, at about the time of the Mexican War.

me when I was coming upon the Mexicans. When I was reconnoitering [surveying enemy territory for information] around Veracruz, their dogs frequently told me by barking when I was approaching them too nearly...."

Lee had been sent to General Winfield Scott's army near Veracruz. And it was almost like a college reunion for the West Point graduate. There he found his friend Captain Joseph E. Johnston (Class of '29), as well as Lieutenant George Gordon Meade ('35), Jubal Early ('37), Lieutenant P. G. T. Beauregard ('38), Lieutenant D. H. Hill ('42), Lieutenant Ulysses S. Grant ('43), and Lieutenant Thomas Jackson ('46). These men would fight side by side to defeat the Mexican army. But one day in the not-too-distant future, they and their fellow soldiers would face one another on opposite sides of the Civil War battlefield.

Lee's first chore was to construct earthworks to protect the batteries, or groups of cannon, that would fire on the city. A crew of sailors was assigned to the project. There was not much time, so Lee pushed them hard. These men, used to fighting on the open seas, were outraged and soon began to complain. Why, they had not enlisted just to dig dirt, they cried. Especially under the orders of a "landlubber."

The sailors' captain protested this outrage. "The boys don't want any dirt to hide behind," he said; "they only want to get at the enemy; and after you have finished your banks we will not stay behind them, we will get up on top where we can have a fair fight."

But Lee had his orders. He pressed on with the work with curses ringing in his ears.

When the Mexican guns began firing, however, the sailors were quick to hide behind their walls of dirt. Later the captain of the sailors apologized to Lee: "Well I reckon you were right. I suppose the dirt *did* save some of my boys from being killed or wounded...." But he added, "The fact is, Captain, I don't like the land fighting anyway. It ain't clean."

The fighting had begun the morning of March 24, 1847. Lee's brother, Sydney Smith Lee, was also there, and they faced their first battle together. Later Lee wrote home about his brother and the battle: "I stood by his gun when I was not wanted elsewhere. Oh, I felt awfully, and am at a loss what I should have done had he been cut down before me. I thank God that he was saved. He preserved his usual cheerfulness, and I could see his white teeth through all the smoke and din of the fire. I had placed three thirty-two and three sixty-eight pound guns in position.... Their fire was terrific, and the shells thrown from our battery were constant and regular discharges, so beautiful in their flight and so destructive in their fall. It was awful! My heart bled for the inhabitants. The soldiers I did not care so much for, but it was terrible to think of the women and children."

On March 26, the Mexicans called for a truce. They formally surrendered Veracruz on March 29, 1847.

Meanwhile, Santa Anna's army of more than 12,000 men was waiting at a pass through the mountains called Cerro Gordo. They seemed invincible. Roads were cut through the mountains, and artillery was hauled by rope up steep slopes. The battle on April 18 was brief; the U.S. Army stormed the pass, and the Mexicans soon laid down their arms. General Scott praised Lee in his official dispatches following the battle: "I am impelled to make special mention of the services of Captain R. E. Lee, engineers. This officer, greatly distinguished at the siege of Veracruz, was again indefatigable [tireless] during these operations, in reconnaissance as daring as laborious, and of the utmost value. Nor was he less conspicuous in planting batteries, and in conducting columns to their stations under the heavy fire of the enemy."

Lee proved himself again and again on the long march to Mexico City. One night Lee volunteered to cross a huge plain of broken lava called *pedregal* to take battle plans to General Scott. He traveled on foot for miles through the rain, with only the flash of lightning to show him the way. He arrived at headquarters, then led troops back over the same route. General Scott called it "the greatest feat of physical and mental courage performed by any individual, in my knowledge, pending the campaign."

Before reaching Mexico City, the army had to deal with Chapultepec, a steep ridge that the Mexicans had reinforced with walls and mines. Scott's men charged the hill repeatedly, and at last they succeeded in taking it.

Lee was wounded at Chapultepec. He did not even stop to have his wound attended to, however. He planned to continue in his duties, but he fainted. It was the only time Lee was a casualty of any battle. Before sunrise the next morning, he was back in the saddle and rode with the army to Mexico City.

The final assault on the capital city was difficult and bloody. In the end, the Americans broke the resistance and marched triumphantly to the Halls of Montezuma, the offices of the government. The final peace treaty, called the Treaty of Guadalupe Hidalgo, was signed on February 2, 1848. In it, the Mexican government agreed to give up all of the land that would later become the states of Texas, California, Nevada, and Utah, as well as parts of Arizona, Wyoming, Colorado, and New Mexico. The United States had used its muscle and gotten what it wanted: control of the continent.

Robert E. Lee had scored high at West Point for his technical drawing skills, and he spent the winter of 1847–48 drawing up maps of Mexico City and the surrounding battlefields. It was not until May 21, 1848, that Mexico ratified the treaty that brought peace.

Lee had spent 20 months in Mexico, and he had learned well the lessons of war. He learned to face fire without flinching. He learned the importance of strategy and the value of intelligent gambles. He saw up close the day-to-day workings of an army doing its job.

At 41, Lee was still unknown to the general public, but his reputation within the army was firmly established. General Scott called him "the very best soldier that I ever saw in the field." For his brave service in Mexico, he was promoted to the rank of colonel. At last, in June, he headed home to Virginia.

It had been a long and painful separation from his family, and he and some of the younger children hardly knew each other. Upon his return, his beloved dog Spec was the first to recognize Lee. Robert, Jr., remembered how humiliated he was when his father picked up and hugged Robert's playmate, thinking it was his son. In a letter to his brother Sydney Smith Lee, dated June 30, 1848, Colonel Lee wrote: "Here I am once again, my dear Smith, perfectly surrounded by Mary and her precious children, who seem to devote themselves to staring at the furrows in my face and the white hairs on my head. It is not surprising that I am hardly recognisable to some of the young eyes around me and perfectly unknown to the youngest. But some of the older ones gaze with astonishment and wonder at me, and seem at a loss to reconcile [bring together] what they see and what was pictured in their imagination."

After the war Lee returned to engineering work, strengthening the forts along the Atlantic coast. For a time the family lived in Baltimore, Maryland. Then, on May 28, 1852, Lee received surprising orders: He was assigned to serve as superintendent of West Point. Lee felt unqualified for the job. A further complication was that his son Custis would be one of the cadets in his charge. Lee wrote: "I learn with much regret the determination of the Secretary of War to assign me to that duty, and I fear I cannot realize his expectations in the management of an Institution requiring more skill and experience than I can command." The War Department did not share his doubts, and his orders stood.

So Lee set out to do his best, and earned a reputation as one of the best superintendents West Point ever had. He felt that he and his own family should set an example for the cadets, and he wrote once to his daughter Annie: "I do not know what the Cadets will say if the Superintendent's children do not practice what he demands of them. They will naturally say he had better attend to his own before he corrects other people's children."

Lee took a great interest in all his cadets, and he found punishing them a difficult chore. One day Lee and his son Robert, Jr., were out riding. As they came around a curve in the road, three cadets took a flying leap over a low wall to keep from being seen. They had sneaked off campus, which could earn them demerits. Lee rode on for a minute or two without saying a word. Then he asked his son, "Did you know those young men? But no!—if you did, don't say so." For if Lee knew their names, he would be honor-bound to report them. Then he added with a sigh, "I wish boys would do what is right, it would be so much easier for all of us."

Near the end of his first year at West Point, in April 1853, the Lees learned that Mrs. Custis was very ill. Before Mary could reach Arlington, her mother had died. Lee was as shocked by the death as his wife was. As soon as graduation was over at West Point in July, Lee joined her at Arlington.

Though Lee had always been deeply religious, he had never formally joined the Episcopal church. But now he had seen death on the battlefield. He had been deeply affected by the death of his mother-in-law. And he had become a role model for all the young cadets at West Point. So on July 17, at Christ Church in Alexandria, Robert E. Lee was confirmed in the Episcopal church.

In his role as superintendent, Lee reported directly to Secretary of

War Jefferson Davis, a West Point classmate who would one day command him as president of the Confederacy. West Point at that time was filled with other cadets who would one day stand with Lee or against him in battle, including Lee's nephew Fitzhugh Lee, John B. Hood, James B. McPherson, and William Pender.

Among the cadets who got into trouble during Lee's stay were two outstanding but hot-tempered young men who would be major figures in the Civil War: James Ewell Brown (J. E. B.) Stuart from Virginia, and Philip Henry Sheridan from Ohio. Stuart would jump into a fight at the drop of a hat, which was of course against academy rules. Once he was charged with speaking disrespectfully to a teacher. Lee said in his report: "It is difficult to understand how one of Cadet Stuart's intelligence should have failed to see the impropriety [wrongness] of his course.... [The superintendent] is, however, convinced that Cadet Stuart now sees his fault, and trusts that its further prosecution is not necessary." Later Stuart, who was the same age as Lee's son Custis, became a frequent guest at the Lee home, and Lee developed a fondness and respect for the dashing young cavalryman who would serve him so well in the Civil War.

Lee hated to see any of his cadets fail. He kept up with their work week by week. He wrote personal letters to parents whose sons needed gentle encouragement. Above all, he hated to expel a student. Often when a cadet was in trouble or failing, Lee suggested to the parents that they might allow the young man to resign, to avoid embarrassment.

Of one cadet he said, "I can only regret that one so capable of doing well should have so neglected himself and must now suffer the penalty." The cadet was first in his drawing class, but had not done well in other subjects, and had 136 demerits. On a chemistry exam, when asked to define *silicon*, he said it was a gas. Years later the young man said, "If silicon had chanced to be a gas, I might now be a major-general in the United States Army." The cadet was James McNeill Whistler, who would become a major American painter famous for the painting popularly known as *Whistler's Mother*.

Lee spent nearly three years at West Point, and he loved being near his family. All that was soon to change, however. Settlers and speculators were moving westward, taking over the lands that had belonged to the Native Americans for generations. As these tribes fought to protect their land, more and more soldiers were needed to protect U. S. citizens. More than twenty Indian wars with various tribes took place in the 1850s. In March 1855, Lee was transferred out of engineering into the new Second Cavalry. He was appointed lieutenant colonel reporting to Colonel Albert Sidney Johnston. For Lee, this was not a happy promotion. He was once again separated from his family: This time he was sent to the hot, dusty Texas frontier. For a year and a half, he saw very little fighting and spent most of his time traveling to remote posts to hold court-martial hearings.

Lee had had high hopes for his career following his successes in the Mexican War. He was now nearly 50, and his career seemed to be going nowhere. He saw himself passed over for promotions, making barely enough money to support his large family. In October 1857, his father-in-law died suddenly, leaving him debts, a complicated will to handle, and a run-down estate. The family was "land poor"—they owned a great deal of property but had almost no money for its upkeep. Lee was given two months' leave to go home to Arlington and settle the estate. The job that faced Lee there, however, required a lot more time than that. He had to make repairs on Arlington and make the farm self-supporting again to pay off their debts. His leaves had to be extended for nearly two years to get everything in order. What was even more depressing, Lee found that in his absence, Mary had become half-crippled with painful arthritis and had trouble walking. Most of the children were away in the army or at boarding school. It was a dark time for Lee, and he even considered resigning from the army.

But Lee was about to get an urgent message from the secretary of war. Trouble was brewing in Virginia, in a town called Harpers Ferry.

HARPERS FERRY

"John Brown's body lies a mold'ring in the
grave...his soul is marching on."
FROM A POPULAR NORTHERN CIVIL WAR SONG, SUNG
TO THE TUNE OF THE "BATTLE HYMN OF THE REPUBLIC"

n the rainy morning of October 16, 1859, Lieutenant Jeb Stuart just happened to be sitting in the War Department in Washington with his new invention—"a stout brass hook."

It was a simple enough design, but with it a soldier in battle could more quickly remove his sword and scabbard from his belt and attach it to his saddle as he hurried to mount his horse. A dashing cavalryman himself, Stuart had designed the special hook while on leave after being wounded during one of the many Indian wars in the West. He hoped to sell the patented invention to the army, for he believed it would save time—and lives—during the heat of battle.

Suddenly Secretary of War John B. Floyd received an urgent telegram from the president of the Baltimore and Ohio Railroad. Strangers had taken over a United States arsenal—a building for storage of military weapons and ammunition—in Harpers Ferry, Virginia (now West Virginia). Exactly what was happening was unclear. Rumors were flying that a slave uprising was in the making. Troops were ordered to the scene, and orders were quickly drawn up for Lieutenant Colonel Robert E. Lee to take command.

50

Lee led U.S. troops in quelling abolitionist John Brown's uprising at Harpers Ferry, Virginia.

Stuart volunteered to deliver the sealed orders to his old West Point superintendent in Arlington.

When Lee read the orders, he left for Washington immediately, without even changing out of his civilian clothes.

From Washington, he and Stuart left for Sandy Point, about a mile from Harpers Ferry. They arrived about 10 o'clock that night. There they learned that a man who called himself Smith and an unknown number of followers—blacks and whites—were holding local citizens hostage inside the armory's fire engine house.

But there was reason to suspect the man in charge was John Brown, a tall, gaunt, grizzly-bearded, fanatical abolitionist from Kansas. Abolitionists believed slavery was morally wrong and should be ended immediately—that all slaves should be set free with no compensation to the owners. Brown was known for his fiery speeches and his efforts to free the slaves through the use of force. He advocated an armed uprising and had killed slave-owners in Kansas. Some people said he was crazy; others saw him as a hero. Many believed he was dangerous.

That afternoon, Lee learned that Virginia and Maryland soldiers had killed eight of Brown's men, and three civilians had also been killed in the fighting.

"I made plans to attack...at daylight," Lee wrote in his official report. "But for the fear of sacrificing the lives of some of the gentlemen held by them as prisoners in a midnight assault, I should have ordered the attack at once. Their safety was the subject of painful consideration, and to prevent if possible jeopardizing their lives, I determined to summon the insurgents to surrender."

Lee wrote a letter demanding that the men surrender peacefully, warning that the armory was surrounded and that if he were compelled to take them by force, he could not answer for their safety.

Stuart was the only soldier there who had ever seen John Brown before. Only he would be sure to recognize him. So Lee asked Stuart to deliver the letter under a white flag. If the men inside refused to surrender, Stuart was to wave his cap, and a party of U.S. soldiers would storm the engine house.

In a letter to his mother, Stuart described what happened: "I approached the door in the presence of perhaps two thousand spectators and told Mr. Smith that I had a communication from Colonel Lee. He opened the door about four inches and placed his body against the crack with a cocked carbine in his hand: hence his remark after his capture that he could have wiped me out like a mosquito." Stuart immediately recognized the man as "[John] Brown who had given...so much trouble in Kansas."

"The parley [meeting] was a long one. He presented his propositions in every possible shape and with admirable tact; but it all amounted to this: that the only condition upon which he would surrender was that he and his party should be allowed to escape. Some of his prisoners begged me to ask Colonel Lee to come and see him. I told them that he would never accede to any terms but those he had offered; and as soon as I could tear myself away from their importunities [requests] I left the door and waved my cap."

The Marines attacked, battering in the door with a heavy ladder. Three minutes later it was over. Two more men had been killed. Brown and two others were wounded. All thirteen hostages escaped injury.

Lee wrote in his report that John Brown "avows that his object was the liberation of the slaves of Virginia, and of the whole South; and acknowledges that he has been disappointed in the expectations of aid from the blacks as well as white population, both in the Southern and Northern states. The blacks whom he forced from their homes in this neighborhood, as far as I could learn, gave him no voluntary assistance.... The result proves that the plan was the attempt of a fanatic or madman, which could only end in failure...."

Lee thought Harpers Ferry was only a minor event. But it was like a lighted match starting a brushfire, inflaming Northerners and Southerners on both sides of the slavery issue. Brown revealed that several noted Northerners had given him money and support, and his captors found maps targeting seven other states for freeing slaves. Southerners were shocked by this murderous man who had tried to arm slaves against them. They were outraged at the support he won in the North. Though some Northerners criticized the events at Harpers Ferry at anti-Brown meetings, many admired him as a daring saint. Writer Henry David Thoreau called him "a crucified hero." Harpers Ferry illuminated the increasingly bitter division between North and South.

At his trial Brown spoke with eloquence: "I deny everything but what I have all along admitted: of a design on my part to free slaves.... Had I interfered in the manner which I admit... in behalf of the rich, the powerful, the intelligent, the so-called great... every man in this Court would have deemed it an act worthy of reward rather than punishment... Now, if it is deemed necessary that I should forfeit my life for the furtherance of justice, and mingle my blood further with the blood of my children and with the blood of millions in this slave country whose rights are disregarded by wicked, cruel, and unjust enactments, I say, let it be done."

Brown was convicted of treason and was sentenced to hang on the morning of December 2, 1859. Henry Wadsworth Longfellow wrote in his diary, "This will be a great day in our history, the date of a new Revolution—quite as much needed as the old one." Across the nation church bells rang out, fiery sermons were preached, tempers flared. As Brown left the jail, headed for the gallows, he handed someone a slip of paper:

"I John Brown am now quite *certain* that the crimes of this *guilty* land: will never be purged *away*; but with Blood. I had *as I now think*: vainly flattered myself that without very much bloodshed; it might be done."

WAR BEGINS

"If Virginia stands by the old Union, so will I.
But if she secedes (though I do not believe in
secession as a Constitutional right, nor that there
is a sufficient cause for revolution), then I will
still follow my native state with my sword, and,
if need be, with my life.... These are my
principles, and I must follow them."

LEE, QUOTED BY A FELLOW OFFICER IN TEXAS

On February 10, 1860, Lee once again said goodbye to the Arlington he had worked so hard to restore and to his cherished family. He had been assigned to take command of the Department of Texas, in charge of most of the Southwest. From here he would watch the gathering storm of the Civil War. Here he would be forced to face his own divided feelings.

It was a dark time for Lee. He was 53 years old and had little to show for his 31 years in the army. He was only a lieutenant colonel with a salary of $1,205 a year. He was homesick for his family and worried about his invalid wife and four unmarried daughters, who, like most women of the time, would live at home until they found husbands to support them. He was a good, loyal soldier who had shown his skill in Mexico. But he was not given to self-promotion, and so he watched with quiet frustration as other, less qualified men won the promotions that seemed forever out of his reach. A quiet depression settled over him, and he became increasingly withdrawn. When he learned that spring that his first grandchild had been named after him, Lee wrote his son Rooney: "I wish I could offer him a more worthy name and a better example. He

must elevate the first and make use of the latter to avoid the errors I
have committed."

All around him, soldiers and civilians alike hotly argued the idea
of states breaking away from the Union—known as secession—and
the threat of war as if it were all an entertainment. But Lee was a
man of moderation and reason. He was against slavery and thought
it was a dying institution. He once called it "a moral and political
evil." But he could not support the violent measures used by
abolitionists such as John Brown. Though he had strong loyalties
to his own state, he believed "secession is nothing but revolution."
He felt committed to the United States, founded by his forefathers
and his idol, George Washington. He had spent his life in service to
the army. But his roots were deeply planted in Virginia soil.

"I wish to do what is right," he wrote his son Custis. "I am
unwilling to do what is wrong, either at the bidding of the South
or of the North."

But 1860 was not a year for moderation and reason. The country
was aflame with anger and fear. Too much had been said and done
that could not be erased. The North and South were like jealous
siblings whose fighting escalates far beyond the original quarrel
into a full-blown brawl. But no one, North or South, yet realized
just how bloody this brawl between brothers would become.

"There is nothing in all the dark caves of human passion so cruel
and deadly as the hatred the South Carolinians profess for the
Yankees," a *London Times* correspondent wrote from Charleston.
After Abraham Lincoln was elected president on November 6,
1860, that hatred led to swift action. On December 20, South
Carolina became the first state to break away from the Union, and
one by one, other Southern states followed.

Lee watched these events with a growing sense of doom. On
January 22, 1861, from Fort Macon, Texas, he wrote to his cousin
Markie:

God alone can save us from our folly, selfishness & short-
sightedness. The last accounts seem to show that we have barely
escaped anarchy [lawlessness] to be plunged into civil war. What

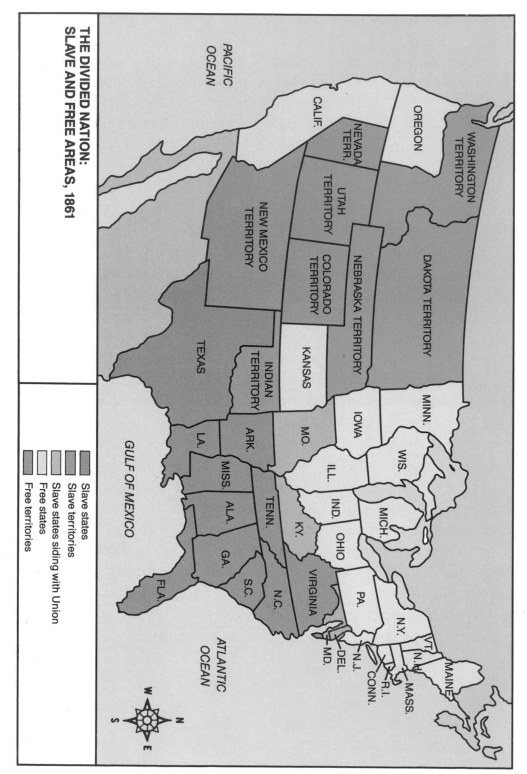

**THE DIVIDED NATION:
SLAVE AND FREE AREAS, 1861**

Slave states
Slave territories
Slave states siding with Union
Free states
Free territories

will be the result I cannot conjecture [guess]. I only see that a fearful calamity is upon us, & fear that the country will have to pass through for its sins a fiery ordeal. I am unable to realize that our people will destroy a government inaugurated by the blood & wisdom of our patriot fathers, that has given us peace & prosperity at home, power & security abroad... I wish to live under no other government, & there is no sacrifice I am not ready to make for the preservation of the Union save that of honor. If a disruption takes place, I shall go back in sorrow to my people & share the misery of my native state, & save in her defence there will one soldier less in the world than now. I wish for no other flag save the 'Star Spangled banner,' & no other air than 'Hail Columbia.' I still hope that the wisdom & patriotism of the nation will yet save it.

Most Southern whites saw their states as strong individual members of a government organization called the United States. They believed that since they no longer agreed with the way the government was being run, they had the right to end their own state's affiliation—to "quit the club." They felt they had the right to allow slavery in their own state if they chose. They also feared that as the North spread its influence westward, Southerners, with their Southern ideas and way of life, would become even more of a minority voice in the government. The states had joined the Union individually, and they believed their states had the freedom and the right to leave individually. Hadn't the colonies themselves made that free choice less than a century ago, when they broke with England?

Most Northerners believed that the whole was bigger than the sum of its parts—that the Union as a whole had become what was most important. A democracy—a government by the people— could not survive if any state or region could just quit any time it did not like a particular law or policy of the government. Secession was the act of a traitor.

Still, some Northerners believed that physical force should not be used to make the Southern states remain in the Union against their will. Horace Greeley, editor of the New York *Tribune*, wrote:

"We hope never to live in a republic whereof one section is pinned to the residue by bayonets."

By February 1, a total of seven states had seceded from the Union: South Carolina, Mississippi, Florida, Alabama, Georgia, Louisiana, and Texas, where Lee was stationed. "May God rescue us from our own acts, save us from selfishness and teach us to love our neighbors as ourselves," Lee wrote.

That month a convention of delegates from the seven seceding states elected Jefferson Davis president of the new Confederate States of America. Lee had little hope for a new government founded by states that insisted upon their individual independence.

Then suddenly, in March, he was relieved of his duties and ordered to report to Washington. A fellow soldier who had come to tell Lee good-bye wrote, "I have seldom seen a more distressed man."

But Virginia had not yet seceded. Virginia could not secede unless voters approved such a resolution at the polls. There were considerable differences between the states of the Deep South that had seceded and the states of the Upper South, which had not. These states—including Virginia, Arkansas, North Carolina, and Tennessee—were not so eager to abandon the Union. Attitudes were different in the Upper South, especially regarding slavery. In the Deep South, nearly 40 percent of white families owned slaves; in the Upper South, it was only about 20 percent.

At Lee's Arlington home, things happened quickly. On April 18, Lee met with his old commander, General Winfield Scott, a fellow Virginian. It was time for all loyal soldiers to declare their loyalty to the Union—or resign. Scott admired Lee and urged him to stay. Several weeks later, Lee was given a commission as permanent colonel in the U.S. Army.

About the same time, he received a letter offering him a position as brigadier general in the army the Confederates were raising. This second offer he ignored.

Then on April 12, the Confederates fired on Fort Sumter, in South Carolina. On April 14, the fort was surrendered to the Confederate Army. Lincoln called for 75,000 troops to stop the

Jefferson Davis, the U.S. senator from Mississippi, became president of the Confederacy.

Confederates. Then came the offer, authorized by Lincoln, for Lee to take command of this huge army that would put an end to the uprising, an end to the possibility of war. It was the chance of a lifetime—a fabulous promotion, authority, the opportunity to use the military skills he had had little use for since Mexico...a chance for glory at the end of a lackluster career.

But the chance had come at the wrong time, the wrong place. Lee struggled with these feelings of mixed loyalty—and with the words of advice he had received from General Scott: "There are times when every officer in the United States service should fully determine what course he will pursue and frankly declare it. No one should continue in government employ without being actively employed."

The next morning, April 19, Lee learned that the Virginia convention had voted to secede. For the elated Virginians around him, it was the end of waiting and indecision, the beginning of independence and glory. But for Lee and many other Virginians who did not wish for secession, it was "the beginning of sorrow."

After a night of private struggle, Lee turned down the offer— and resigned from the United States Army, the only career he had ever known.

Two mornings later, Lee left Arlington, not knowing he would never enter it again. He had been summoned to Richmond, Virginia. There Governor John Letcher offered him a new post: major general in "command of the military and naval forces of Virginia." Lee accepted the job—to lead the defense of his native state—without hesitation. The governor submitted Lee's name to the state convention that night, and Lee's appointment was approved unanimously.

The next day, he went to the state capitol building to formally accept the post. In a speech, John Janney, president of the Virginia convention, said to Lee: "Yesterday, your mother, Virginia, placed her sword in your hand upon the implied condition that we know you will keep to the letter and in spirit, that you will draw it only in her defense, and that you will fall with it in your hand rather than that the object for which it was placed there shall fail."

Thus Lee took his first post in a war he did not wish to fight— and there was little time to lose. President Lincoln's proclamation of April 15—the one that called for 75,000 Union troops—had also included a strong warning to the Southern states. It gave the gathering Southern armies 20 days "to disperse and return peaceably to their respective abodes [homes]." Southern military leaders felt this warning meant that Lincoln would hold off till May 5— then the Union army would begin its attack. If this were true, Lee had less than two weeks left to prepare.

Virginia was the most vulnerable state in the South—its borders reached to Washington, capital of the Union. Lee's first tasks were huge: the appointment of officers, the organization of an army from scratch, preparation of a military defense. But Lee had developed excellent administrative skills while head of West Point. These talents enabled him to quickly organize a staff and fully equip an army of 40,000 men. He set up systems for making weapons and handling supplies. Many plans would have to be made up as he went along, but everything Lee did had a single goal: to create a strong defense.

Neither the North nor the South was in any way prepared militarily for war. Before Lincoln's call for troops, there were only 16,000 soldiers in the entire United States Army. The people were not prepared emotionally for what would happen, either. Few people had ever seen war up close—there were no photographs of past wars, no movies or television broadcasts of what a battlefield was really like. People learned about war from stories of heroism passed down by parents and grandparents, or perhaps from paintings that honored bravery and glorified the life of a soldier. War was something that happened far away, something that brought honor to those who won.

Most people in the North and South thought the war would be over in a matter of months. Northern volunteers were only required to sign up for three months. Both sides believed a battle or two was all it would take to put the other side in its place and decide the matter once and for all.

But after only a few days in Richmond, Robert wrote to Mary, "The war may last ten years." He knew she was not safe in Arlington, their family home overlooking what was now the capital of the enemy. He urged her to pack up the family heirlooms and send them to a safe place, then leave. "Where to go is the difficulty. When the war commences no place will be exempt in my opinion, and indeed all the avenues into the state will be the scene of military operations."

May 5 came and went. The Union army made no move. Still, when Robert learned Mary was still at Arlington, he insisted that she leave "the scene of war. It may burst upon you at any time. It is sad to think of the devastation, if not ruin it may bring upon a spot so endeared to us. But God's will be done. We must be resigned."

On May 14, 1861, Mary Lee left Arlington. On May 23, the people of Virginia formally approved the ordinance of secession. The very next day, Union troops took over Arlington.

Now that Virginia had formally seceded, the state's army became part of the Confederate army. Lee accepted a lower rank than he had in the Union, that of brigadier general, without complaint. Then the Confederate government moved its headquarters from Montgomery, Alabama, to Richmond, Virginia. Their new enemy's capital—Washington, D.C.—was a mere 100 miles away.

Lee was on good terms with the new president, Jefferson Davis. He continued his work of incorporating Virginia forces into the Confederate army. But he wrote his wife, "I do not know what my position will be. I should like to retire to private life if I could be with you and the children, but if I can be of any service to the State or her cause, I must continue."

The first year of the war was to be, for Lee, one of frustrating paperwork and politics, rather than action on the field of battle. He advised President Davis on military issues, and there was office work to be taken care of, but often Lee had little to do.

The streets of Richmond were turning into a street fair as excited volunteers from throughout the South thronged into the capital, each group proudly wearing its own uniform. There were long-haired Western-outfitted Texans on horseback, Maryland Zouaves dressed in exotic costumes of orange and blue, Georgia boys in coarse gray homespun, hats with plumes, jackets with braid, white gloves, and solid brass buttons. John Beauchamp Jones wrote in *A Rebel War Clerk's Diary* that "the ladies are postponing all engagements until their lovers have fought the Yankees.... They go in crowds to the fairgrounds where the 1st S.C. Vols. are encamped, showering upon them their smiles.... They wine them and cake them—and they deserve it." It was all like some kind of gay party or spring festival.

Then word came in early June that Union forces under General Irvin McDowell would soon make a move at Manassas Junction,

Virginia, near a creek called Bull Run. The North would remember this battle as the first battle of Bull Run. In the South it would be known as the battle of Manassas. Throughout the war the South and North often gave different names to the same battles.

Lee asked to go to the field, but President Davis thought it was more important for Lee to stay at headquarters—while Davis himself went to witness the battle. With his West Point training and military experience in Mexico, Davis was a well-trained professional soldier. He did not like to delegate responsibility, and he probably would have been much happier serving as secretary of war rather than president of the Confederacy. This would prove to be one of his weaknesses throughout the war.

On July 21, 1861, the Southern and Northern armies—overconfident and undertrained—faced each other for the first time in a major battle. And a strange day it was. Hundreds of gentlemen and ladies and children from Washington, including many congressmen, had driven out in carriages and buggies as if they were watching a parade. Apparently believing the Union soldiers would soon send the Rebels running, they spread out their picnic baskets and blankets on the hillside and tried to see what was going on.

General Irvin McDowell's 30,000 men faced about 22,000 led by General Joseph E. Johnston and P. G. T. Beauregard. The battle was one of confusion as the field of inexperienced young men tried to figure out how to shoot one another without getting shot full of holes themselves. "Forward to Richmond" was the Union army's call, and at one point it seemed that they would indeed break through the Confederate line. Then the South's Brigadier General Barnard Bee saw a group of Virginia soldiers holding their ground, with General Thomas J. Jackson standing tall and returning Union fire.

"There is Jackson standing like a stone wall!" Bee shouted. "Rally behind the Virginians!" The call helped hearten the troops. From that moment on the bearded soldier would be known as "Stonewall" Jackson. At another point, soldiers in Union blue held their fire when they saw a group of men wearing blue uniforms. Too late they learned that these were blue-suited Confederates leading a counterattack.

WILLITS BRANCH LIBRARY

Though both sides were inept, the Southerners had the spirit of defending home territory to their advantage. When 9,000 Confederate reinforcements showed up, they soon had the Union running. The picnickers watching the returning army panicked and hurried into their carriages, clogging the road to Washington that the army wanted to use. A stray Confederate shell exploded near a bridge and overturned a carriage, and the crowds fled back to Washington in terror.

Bull Run, or Manassas, was the nation's first taste of real warfare. On the Union side, 2,896 men were killed, wounded, or missing; on the Confederate side, the number was 1,982. The Northerners were shocked. They had expected a quick end to the rebellion. Instead they had suffered a humiliating defeat. Southerners were euphoric over their victory, sure now that the North could be beaten easily.

Lee's military organization and his strategy of concentrating troops at Manassas had in fact contributed to the success of the battle. But he wrote his wife that he was "mortified" to have been absent from that "struggle for my home and neighbors."

Lee's first chance to be involved in the field was in western Virginia—and it was a disaster. The Union's General George Brinton McClellan was causing trouble in a region where many counties had voted against secession. Lee was sent not as a commander of troops, but as an adviser or coordinator. When he arrived in the mountains he found total disorganization. It had been raining for weeks. There was an outbreak of measles among the soldiers—and an outbreak of jealousy among several of the officers. Here Lee showed a weakness that would haunt him throughout the war: He was too much of a gentleman—too polite to indulge in quarreling, too courteous to clash with his subordinates. His way was to suggest or advise rather than to command. Lee's gentlemanly manner did not endear him to the locals. The situation dragged into October and developed into a standoff. Then on October 24, 1861, the overwhelming majority of people in the western counties voted to secede from Virginia to form their own state—West Virginia—and rejoin the Union.

Lee returned to an enraged outpouring of public criticism. The Richmond papers called him "Granny Lee." Lee's nephew Fitzhugh Lee wrote later of this time: "Men apparently wise shook their heads and said he had been overrated as a soldier; that he had relied upon a 'showy presence' and a 'historic name,' and that he was 'too tender of blood' and leaned too much to the engineer side of a military question, preferring rather to dig entrenchments than to fight."

President Davis did not lose faith in him, however, and publicly supported him. He said, "He came back carrying the heavy weight of defeat, and unappreciated by the people he served...Yet, through all this, with a magnanimity rarely equalled, he stood in silence, without defending himself or allowing others to defend him, for he was unwilling to offend any one who was wearing a sword and striking blows for the Confederacy."

Lee acquired two things in western Virginia. One was the neat grandfatherly white beard that would become his trademark. The other was a gray horse named Jeff Davis. Lee bought him for $2,000 and gave him a new name—Traveller. This was the horse that would take Lee into battle—and carry him safely out—through four long years of war, becoming his favorite of all the horses he ever had.

President Davis now put Lee in command of all Confederate forces along the southeastern coast. The North was trying to blockade Southern ports by sailing old ships filled with stone into the harbors and blowing them up, thus blocking traffic in and out. In this way the South would be cut off from the support of foreign trade goods. Lee traveled up and down the coast inspecting the harbors. He fortified the defenses at Charleston, South Carolina, and Savannah, Georgia, and raised 25,000 troops. Lee's work significantly strengthened the Southern defense, though it was work that did not attract public attention as fighting on the battlefield did.

Lee faced the first Christmas of the war homesick for Arlington and for his family. To his wife he wrote, "As to our old home, if not destroyed, it will be difficult ever to be recognized...With the number of troops encamped around it...it is vain to think of its being in a habitable [fit to live in] condition. I fear, too, books, furniture and the relics of Mount Vernon will be gone. It is better to make up our minds to a general loss. They cannot take away the remembrances of the spot and the memories of those that to us rendered [made] it sacred.... In the absence of a home, I wish I could purchase 'Stratford.' That is the only other place that I could go to...that would inspire me with feelings of pleasure and local love.... I wonder if it is for sale and at how much."

To one of his daughters he wrote, "Among the calamities of war, the hardest to bear, perhaps is the separation of families and friends.... Your old home, if not destroyed by our enemies, has been so desecrated that I cannot bear to think of it. I should have preferred it to have been wiped from the earth...rather than to have been degraded by the presence of those who revel in the ill they do for their own selfish purposes. You see what a poor sinner I am, and how unworthy to possess what was given me; for that reason it has been taken away. I pray for a better spirit, and that the hearts of our enemies may be changed."

It had been a sad year for Lee—perhaps the worst year of his entire life. So much that he held dear seemed to have suffered irreparable damage—the country, his home, his career. But the new year was but a few days away, and in the year 1862, everything would change.

7

Lee's Army of Northern Virginia

"Pope...lacked imagination, except in his
dispatches.... He had no conception that his
adversaries would cheerfully accept risks to
achieve great ends; he had never dreamt of a
general who would deliberately divide his
army..."

COLONEL G. F. R. HENDERSON,
BIOGRAPHER OF JACKSON,
ON POPE'S DEFEAT BY LEE

t was March 1862, and the reality of war had settled into
the country. The pretty fantasies of war had been dashed
by death rolls—and fear of what was to come.

When Lee returned to Richmond he found the Confederate
government confused and without leadership, and the people
suffering from low morale. Both North and South were still
floundering in their inexperience, hampered by slow-moving
generals and mixed-up strategies. But the North was beginning to
take the upper hand. The Confederates' dashing early victory at
Manassas had led to a naive overconfidence that they could easily
"whip" the larger, better-equipped Northern armies. But Union
soldiers were scoring victories in Kentucky, Tennessee, North
Carolina, and Mississippi. The South's lack of manufacturing was
now painfully clear, as supplies of ammunition were already
running low.

Up until now, the Southern army had been made up of
volunteers. Now the Confederates were running short of men. In
April 1862, the Confederate Congress passed the first conscription
act—the first draft—in American history. All white men between
the ages of 18 and 35 could be called to fight—but there were many

ways to get out of serving. For example, anyone who owned more than twenty slaves could not be forced to enlist. Bad health was another exemption, and suddenly rheumatism, a painful disease of the joints, became a very common disease—and popular excuse.

Now Richmond itself—the capital of the Confederacy—was in danger. The Union army was closing in from three sides: There were armies in the Shenandoah Valley of Virginia, troops moving in from Fredericksburg, 50 miles north, and General George B. McClellan just 7 miles away down the James River. The South's defense rested in the hands of Confederate General Joseph E. Johnston. But Johnston ignored advice from Richmond and kept most of his own ideas secret. What's more, he seemed incapable of doing anything decisive to stop the advancing armies.

There was even talk between Davis and his other advisers of abandoning Richmond. Lee was appalled, and he shamed Davis and his cabinet members with his slow deliberate words: "Richmond must not be given up—it shall not be given up."

Though tied to a desk in Richmond, Lee made a decisive move that set the stage for the battle that was to come. He recognized the military daring in General Thomas "Stonewall" Jackson. Jackson was an unlikely hero, but Lee managed to convince Davis to reinforce Jackson's unit so that he could attack Union forces in the Shenandoah Valley. This would force a second arm of the Union army to pull back from Fredericksburg in defense of Washington. Then there would only be McClellan to deal with.

In May 1862, Jackson pulled off an incredible maneuver that students of military strategy study to this day. Outnumbered, Jackson lost the first battle against troops led by James Shields at the northern end of the valley. When reinforcements arrived, instead of pressing north again, Jackson went south, and surprised Union troops led by Lieutenant Robert Milroy camped in the mountains at McDowell, Virginia, near the southern end of the valley. Turning north again, Jackson's troops charged up the valley and sent Union troops running all the way out of the valley and up the Potomac River. Again Jackson turned around and headed south. This time, two Union armies were closing in from the east and west to trap him at the southern end of the valley. They never met.

General McClellan (center) was repeatedly outwitted by Lee in the spring of 1862.

Jackson's troops raced down the valley between them. Turning to the west, they beat Major General John C. Frémont's troops out of the valley at Cross Keys on June 8. Turning to the east, they beat Shields's troops out of the valley at Port Republic on June 9. The Shenandoah Valley belonged to the Confederacy.

Meanwhile, Johnston had retreated across the Chickahominy River and allowed McClellan's troops to follow him without a fight. Unable to sit still, Lee rode out through the dark night to see for himself what was happening. There he met President Davis, who had also gone out to meet Johnston face to face. They were met by lines of wounded soldiers retreating from a battle that was in danger of being lost. The battle that began on May 31 would be called Four Oaks in the North and Seven Pines in the South. Neither side would claim a clear-cut victory.

Then Johnston was wounded. As Davis and Lee rode back to the capital, the sounds of that day's battle dying in the night, Davis made a decision that would change the face of the war. He wrote later: "When riding from the field of battle with General Robert E. Lee... I informed him that he would be assigned to the command of the army... and that he could make his preparations as soon as he reached his quarters, as I should send the order to him as soon as I arrived at mine."

After a year of war, Lee was thrust into the thick of things to take over an army in the midst of a battle. He had finally gotten the chance to show what he could do. He immediately went to work reorganizing the army; the many small groups from all over the South who were loyal to their own hometown band must become one large army—the Army of Northern Virginia.

Lee's appointment drew immediate ridicule. The public knew Lee as the man who had lost western Virginia. The *Richmond Examiner* called him "evacuating Lee, who has never risked a single battle with the invader." Many in the army voiced their opposition.

But Lee's quick action would soon change that.

Lee ordered the digging of defensive earthworks around Richmond, which earned him the nickname "King of Spades." Behind these barriers, a few soldiers could put up an effective defense, freeing up many more for offensive maneuvers. Then Lee quickly sent Jeb Stuart and a thousand cavalrymen out to determine the exact size and location of McClellan's army. Four days later Stuart returned—in what Lee called "a brilliant exploit": He had daringly circled 150 miles around McClellan's entire army base without capture, and brought back valuable military information.

McClellan did not expect to be attacked, and he had scattered his army from the Chickahominy River to the mouth of the James River. In a series of battles called the Battles of the Seven Days, Lee sent Union troops running: at Mechanicsville, Gaines's Mill, Savage's Station, White Oak Swamp, Frayser's Farm, Malvern Hill. Soon McClellan's troops were entrenched on the other side of the James River.

In only one month Lee had reawakened the war. He had revived the Confederate spirit. He had stopped the Union advance and saved Richmond from invasion, though the cost had been about 20,000 Confederate soldiers. He had given the North its first real adversary. Any hopes that the conflict would soon be over quickly died.

Lincoln ordered General John Pope and his army of 43,000 to reinforce McClellan's 90,000. A ruthless man and a boaster, Pope said, "I have come from the West where we have always seen the backs of our enemies; from an army whose business has been to seek out the adversary and to beat him when he was found."

Lee had only 60,000 troops. Yet as he faced the possibility of an army more than twice that size, he made a daring offensive move few military leaders would have chosen in similar circumstances: He divided his troops. He sent Stonewall Jackson and 25,000 men into the Shenandoah Valley, ordering Jackson to swing around and attack Pope from the rear.

On August 9, Jackson's men surprised General Nathaniel Banks's troops and a section of Pope's army at Cedar Mountain. Jackson then traveled 50 miles in two days to reach a Union supply depot at Manassas Junction, at Pope's rear. Jackson attacked the depot, attracting Pope's attention.

Pope swung his army around and came after Jackson. But he could not find him. By the time his men reached Manassas, Jackson's army had disappeared. In fact, Jackson had repositioned his men on the Bull Run battlefield, where the Confederates had won one of the war's first battles.

On August 29, Pope finally found him. He ordered his men to attack. Pope had the larger army, but by now they were exhausted from hunting down Jackson. Still, they wore down the Confederate troops in hard fighting. At day's end, Pope believed he had won the battle. Pope was so confident of victory that he wired Washington that the enemy was on the retreat.

But the second battle of Bull Run, as it would come to be known in the North (the South would call it Second Manassas), was hardly over. Lee had planned a crushing second strike, and this he now carried out. On August 30, while Jackson's men were still harassing Pope's army, Lee attacked from the rear. The Union army was devastated. Lee's army suffered 9,000 casualties, but the Union lost 16,000 men, as well as a large amount of supplies. Lee had won a major victory, and Pope was disgraced.

Following the battle, Lee rode his horse Traveller across the field. A captain stepped up and said, "General, here is some one who wants to speak to you."

Lee looked down at a young artillery man, who stood with sponge-staff in hand, ready to swab out the barrel between firings. His clothes were ragged and stained with red dirt, his face and hands black with the powder of battle.

"Well, my man," said Lee, "what can I do for you?"

"Why, General, don't you know me?" said the man.

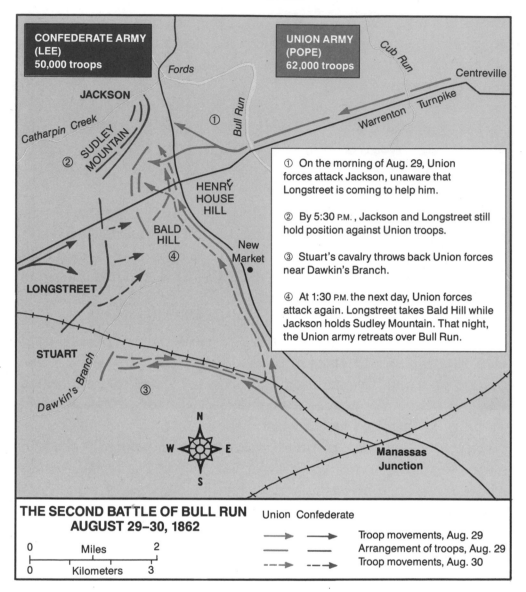

CONFEDERATE ARMY (LEE)
50,000 troops

UNION ARMY (POPE)
62,000 troops

① On the morning of Aug. 29, Union forces attack Jackson, unaware that Longstreet is coming to help him.

② By 5:30 P.M., Jackson and Longstreet still hold position against Union troops.

③ Stuart's cavalry throws back Union forces near Dawkin's Branch.

④ At 1:30 P.M. the next day, Union forces attack again. Longstreet takes Bald Hill while Jackson holds Sudley Mountain. That night, the Union army retreats over Bull Run.

THE SECOND BATTLE OF BULL RUN
AUGUST 29–30, 1862

Union Confederate

Troop movements, Aug. 29
Arrangement of troops, Aug. 29
Troop movements, Aug. 30

0 — Miles — 2
0 — Kilometers — 3

It was Lee's son Robert, who had fought alongside Jackson. Lee was amused by his son's appearance, but glad to see that he had made it safely through the battle.

In 10 weeks Lee had turned the tables. Before, Richmond had almost been lost. Now Washington stood in danger.

Lee grabbed at this new opportunity. He knew that the North had a stronger, better-equipped army. With its major ports and

factories, it would easily outlast the South in terms of supplies and ammunition. But he also knew that with his latest successes, the Northern public was growing tired of the war.

"We cannot afford to be idle," he told President Davis, "and though weaker than our opponents in men and military equipments [sic], we must endeavor to harass if we cannot destroy them."

So far, most of the battles had been fought on Southern land. But now Lee decided that his best chance for ending the war was to give the North a taste of the fighting, a chance to see and feel, up close, the roar of battle and the pain of invasion. To make the North feel that keeping the Southern states in the Union was not worth the price. Lee also hoped a victory in the North would gain foreign recognition of the new Confederate nation. Lee made plans to take the war into the North's backyard.

BAD LUCK RUINS A GOOD IDEA

"You all must do what you can to help drive these
people back."

ROBERT E. LEE TO HIS SON AT ANTIETAM

The hungry, dusty, ragged soldiers plunged into the cool
shallow waters of the Potomac River. As they splashed
their way across, their spirits soared. By the time they
crawled up the muddy banks on the other side they began to cheer.
For the Potomac was the boundary line—the Southern army had
crossed over into Northern territory for the first time in the war.
The regimental bands began to play:

> Thou wilt not cower in the dust
> Maryland, My Maryland
> Thy beaming sword shall never rust
> Maryland, My Maryland

On September 5 and 6, 1862, Lee led more than 55,000 hungry,
half-dressed, poorly armed Confederates across the river in his bold
strike into Northern territory. He chose Maryland for several
reasons. The move would be a direct threat to Washington and
Baltimore and would pull Union troops away from Richmond—
and away from Lee's supply lines bringing sorely needed food and
clothes. Also, Maryland was a state of mixed loyalties. It was a

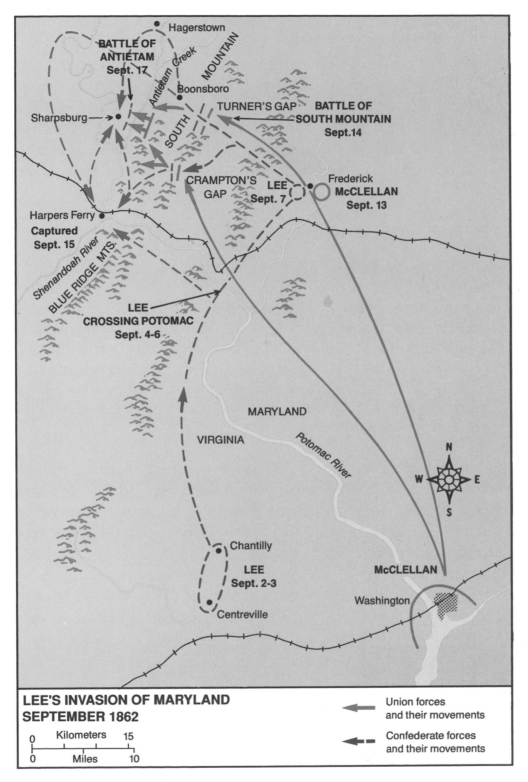

**LEE'S INVASION OF MARYLAND
SEPTEMBER 1862**

Kilometers 15
0

Miles 10
0

Union forces
and their movements

Confederate forces
and their movements

slave-holding state, and many believed its people had been held in the Union against their will. Perhaps their sympathy with the Southern cause would now inspire them to join forces with the invading Southern army. Lee was in sore need of recruits.

But as the ragged army entered the town of Frederick, they received a mixed reaction. Some women rushed out with food and drink for the hungry men. Others held their noses at the dirty, sometimes shoeless soldiers and waved the Union flag in their faces.

On September 8, Lee had a circular printed up to tell the people of Maryland what he planned to do:

> No constraint upon your free will is intended; no intimidation will be allowed within the limits of this army, at least. Marylanders shall once more enjoy their ancient freedom of thought and speech. We know no enemies among you, and will protect all, of every opinion. It is for you to decide your destiny freely and without constraint. This army will respect your choice, whatever it may be; and while the Southern people will rejoice to welcome you to your natural position among them, they will only welcome you when you come of your own free will.

Lee also felt that he was in a good position, with his recent successes and his threatening position in Maryland, to offer the federal government a proposal for ending the war. He wrote to President Davis suggesting that "the Government of the Confederate States... propose to that of the United States the recognition of our independence.... Such a proposition coming from us at this time, could in no way be regarded as suing for peace; but, being made when it is in our power to inflict injury upon our adversary, would show conclusively to the world that our sole object is the establishment of our independence and the attainment of an honorable peace."

Davis never acted upon the advice, however, and Lee prepared for battle.

Lee faced problems every step of the way. Food supplies were running out. Desertions were up. Many soldiers, more than happy to defend their homeland from Northern attack, did not want to risk their lives to invade the North. As many as 10,000 soldiers now fell back or quit the army entirely.

Lee's first action was to send Jackson toward Harpers Ferry to get rid of Union troops that might block supplies coming up the Shenandoah Valley. Lee himself prepared to march to Pennsylvania. One of his officers, Brigadier General John G. Walker, expressed surprise at the move.

"Are you acquainted with General McClellan?" Lee asked. "He is an able general, but a very cautious one. His enemies among his own people think him too much so. His army is in a very demoralized and chaotic condition, and will not be prepared for offensive operations—or he will not think it so—for three or four weeks. Before that time I hope to be on the Susquehanna [river flowing from New York State through Pennsylvania and Maryland]."

Lee's plan was daring but well thought out. He had not expected, however, the accident that undid all his strategy. On September 9, he sent Special Order 191, which included details of his plan, to all division commanders who would take part. Somehow an extra copy was sent to A. P. Hill, and since it was not needed, an unknown officer used it to wrap up three cigars. Unfortunately, that officer dropped the wrapped cigars as they were leaving camp, and the bundle was found when the Union troops entered the camp on September 13. Soon McClellan knew exactly what Lee was going to do, and he pursued his foe with an army of 90,000 men.

Jackson took Harpers Ferry on September 15, then hurried with most of his troops to join forces with Lee on the hilly farmland between Antietam Creek and the Potomac River at a town called Sharpsburg. This would be called the battle of Antietam in the North, the battle of Sharpsburg in the South. Lee had at most 40,000 men, but he decided to stand and fight.

Mist covered the fields at dawn on September 17. As the haze lifted like a curtain on a stage, the battle began.

Wave after wave of Union soldiers advanced upon the Southerners. Hundreds of cannon roared throughout the day, nearly

General D.H. Hill led the southern wing of Lee's army in the maneuvers leading up to Antietam.

blocking out the screams of horses and men. Rows and rows of young men fell to the ground; still others came to take their place.

At one point Lee's son Robert, Jr., a gunner, approached his father, who was pleased to find him well. "General," he said, "are you going to send us in again?"

"Yes, my son," he replied. "You all must do what you can to help drive these people back."

Many times that day it looked as if Union troops would completely overrun their opponents. Then A. P. Hill arrived from Harpers Ferry with reinforcements, and the South managed to hold. As night fell on one of the bloodiest days of the war, the sounds of battle gradually disappeared. Things were at a standstill.

On both sides the casualties were heavy; the dead and wounded littered the field. In one day, the South had lost more than 10,000 men out of 40,000. The North had lost 12,000 out of 75,000. Still, that night, to the surprise of his officers, Lee decided he would not retreat. He would stand and face another day of battle.

The next morning dawned and the Southern army waited expectantly. But the North seemed unwilling to start the fighting. The whole day passed without a shot. Lee knew that time was not on his side. His army could stand and fight, but was too weakened to strike a decisive offensive blow. If he waited too long, Union reinforcements would arrive and overwhelm him. Reluctantly, under cover of darkness, Lee ordered his men back over the Potomac into Virginia. He watched for signs of Union troops, but McClellan, cautious as ever, did not pursue them. Lee sat on Traveller, watching until the last soldier safely crossed the river.

Troops patrol a hilltop after the Battle of Antietam. A single grave lies beneath a lone tree.

A High Price to Pay

"The enemy will make every effort to crush us
between now and June, and it will require all
our strength to resist him."

ROBERT E. LEE,
IN A LETTER TO JEFFERSON DAVIS

Lee quickly set about restoring his tattered army with rest, food, and clothing. He took action to gather up deserters and bring in more recruits. He divided his army into two corps, one under James Longstreet and the other under Stonewall Jackson, who had become a trusted right-hand man. "My opinion of the merits of General Jackson has been greatly enhanced during his expedition," Lee wrote. "He is true, honest and brave; has a single eye to the good of the service, and spares no exertion to accomplish his object."

Winter would soon be setting in, and Lee looked forward to a break in the fighting, as bad roads and weather usually made it impractical to keep huge bodies of men warm, fed, and on the move. But Washington was pushing for action.

The battle of Antietam had been a turning point in the war. At the outset Lee had hoped a Confederate victory would bring European recognition and support. Instead, his defeat gave the North a new weapon. As early as July 1862, President Lincoln had written a draft of a proclamation abolishing slavery. His cabinet, however, had urged him not to issue it. Secretary of State William

Seward said it would be seen in Europe "as the last measure of an exhausted government, a cry for help...our last shriek on the retreat." So Lincoln waited.

Now the Union was basking in what it believed was a decisive victory at Antietam. The time was right. On September 22—only five days after Antietam—Lincoln issued the Emancipation Proclamation. It stated "that on the 1st day of January, A.D. 1863, all persons held as slaves within any State...in rebellion against the United States shall be then, thenceforward, and forever free."

The Emancipation Proclamation was a curious announcement, for it was mostly symbolic. With it, Lincoln freed the slaves in Confederate states—places where the federal government was at this point powerless. But it did not free slaves in the states that were still part of the Union. Strict abolitionists were angry—they believed the proclamation did almost nothing. Many Northern politicians and army officers condemned it. Southerners were outraged that this "foreign" government still dared to meddle in their affairs.

Still, in the long run, the Emancipation Proclamation did what Lincoln had hoped it would do: It added a new moral cause to the war. No longer was the war being fought only over the issue of a state's right to leave the Union. Now it was also a battle for freedom.

After issuing the proclamation, Lincoln brought in a new general to replace McClellan and take over the Army of the Potomac—to have a go at the Southern general who could not be defeated. His name was General Ambrose E. Burnside. He was remembered for the long whiskers he wore, which became known as "burnsides," and eventually "sideburns." Burnside did not want the job, and he would soon prove to be no match for General Lee.

In November, Burnside's army headed south, 125,000 soldiers strong. When word reached Lee, he moved troops into the heights of Fredericksburg, Virginia, overlooking the Rappahannock River. Union troops were already in position on the opposite shore. Lee wrote to his wife: "He [Burnside] threatens to bombard Fredericksburg, and the noble spirit displayed by its citizens, par-

WILLITS BRANCH LIBRARY

ticularly the women and children, has elicited my highest admiration. They have been abandoning their homes, night and day, during all this inclement weather, cheerfully and un-complainingly, with only such assistance as our wagons and ambulances could afford, women, girls, children, trudging through the mud and bivouacking [camping out] in the open fields."

But for many days bad weather and poor administration on Burnside's part delayed action, giving Lee time to summon Jackson and his troops for added support.

On the morning of December 11, a heavy mist only partially concealed what Burnside had been waiting for: He had received supplies for creating pontoon bridges across the river at several points to allow his soldiers to enter the city. Pontoons—flat wooden boats—were put in the water side by side to support wood boards nailed down to make a bridge. It had taken a week to get the pontoons by train, and work had been delayed. Confederate sharpshooters pelted Union soldiers as they worked to get the pontoons in place across the rain-swollen Rappahannock. Despite the odds, Burnside seemed unable to change the plan he had already set in motion, an action that would come to be known as "Burnside's Blunder."

By December 13, more than 80,000 Union soldiers had entered the city. Just above them 75,000 Confederates were ready and waiting, some protected by newly dug breastworks, many en-trenched behind stone walls in Marye's Heights.

The battle of Fredericksburg began. Confederate artillery roared as Union soldiers attempted again and again to march up the hill. Each time they were thrown back. Burnside's only idea seemed to be head-on attack. Six times the Union troops charged straight into enemy fire and certain death. But the Confederates' stronghold could not be broken.

At one point a Confederate charge routed some Union troops from the woods with their high rebel yell, described by a Union chaplain as an "unearthly, fiendish yell, such as no other troops or civilized beings ever uttered." Lee, watching from a nearby hill,

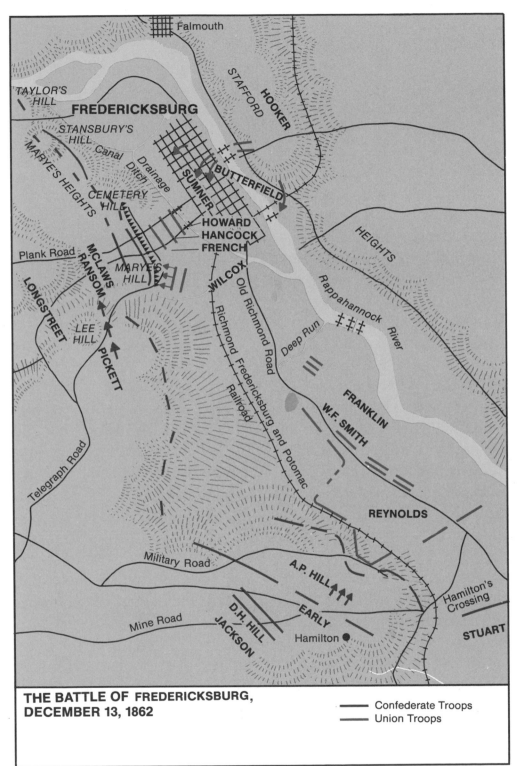

THE BATTLE OF FREDERICKSBURG, DECEMBER 13, 1862

——— Confederate Troops
——— Union Troops

turned to Longstreet and said, "It is well that war is so terrible—we should grow too fond of it!"

When the sun set on the horrible slaughter, the ground was covered with the dead and the dying. Bodies froze to the cold icy ground. Burnside had no choice but to withdraw his troops back across the river. Lee wrote to his wife of the Union retreat, "They went as they came—in the night. They suffered heavily as far as the battle went, but it did not go far enough to satisfy me. Our loss was comparatively slight, and I think will not exceed two thousand. The contest will have now to be renewed, but on what field I cannot say." In fact, Rebel casualties were 5,309—but that was small compared to the Union's loss of 12,653 men. Once again Lee had bested a Northern general. Burnside himself asked to be replaced.

In the South spirits soared. Lee had more than made up for his failure at Antietam, and once again many Southerners believed that Lee had a shot at ending the war soon. Lee himself did not share their feelings. On the last day of 1862, Lee wrote: "The war is not yet ended. The enemy is still numerous and strong, and the country demands of the army a renewal of its heroic efforts in her behalf." The economics of the war frightened him more than all the enemy's armies. The Union seemed able to easily replace every fallen soldier, and its supplies seemed endless. In the South, everything was in short supply. Many photographers of the time show dead Confederate soldiers lying on the battlefield shoeless— their boots were so needed by soldiers who had to continue the fight.

Lee tried to warn President Davis and his cabinet about the serious lack of food and supplies. But the Confederate leaders were too elated by Lee's successes and their dreams of victory to take action.

Meanwhile, another battle was shaping up in Tennessee. On the last day of 1862, Confederate General Braxton Bragg met Union General William S. Rosecrans along the Stones River near Murfreesboro. Though the three days of fighting were more or less a draw, Bragg withdrew. It was a small victory for the North, but it gave it control of much of Tennessee—and a view of the Deep South.

Lee's Army of Northern Virginia, however, saw little action the winter of 1862–63, partly because the weather was so bad. Lee wrote his family in February: "We are in a liquid state... Up to our knees in mud, and what is worse, on short rations for men and beasts. This keeps me miserable. I am willing to starve myself but cannot bear my men or horses to be pinched."

Lee was becoming increasingly frustrated over the failure of Davis and the Confederate Congress to help him increase his ranks. "The enemy will make every effort to crush us between now and June, and it will require all our strength to resist him."

Lincoln, however, was also having trouble. The people in the North were growing weary of the war. For many, the beautiful images of patriotic battle had been replaced by the knowledge of how terrible life on the battlefield really was. Enlistments were down. Desertions were increasing. Many troops had signed up for two-year stints in 1861, and now their assignments were up. In January 1863, Lincoln at last began to allow the use of blacks in the army. Wherever Union soldiers had gone, fleeing ex-slaves had followed them, looking for protection. The government had set up refugee camps and used them for labor. Now Lincoln would use them to help fill his need for troops.

At first many Union soldiers were against the idea of black soldiers. Though they were fighting for the idea of freedom for black slaves, most whites in the North still carried personal prejudices as strong as those of Southern whites. Many white Union soldiers did not want to fight alongside African Americans. Soon, however, they saw some advantages. African Americans fought in all-black regiments—but they were led by whites, so this gave more enlisted white men a chance to be officers. Furthermore, every black soldier in the field saved one more white from having to die in battle.

More than 150,000 African Americans wore Union uniforms in the war. Most of these soldiers actually served as workers or cooks, but many African American regiments saw action. General Benjamin Butler, an abolitionist, used many black troops because, he said, "I knew that they would fight more desperately than any white troops, in order to prevent capture, because they knew... if captured they would be returned to slavery." Though the use of African Americans by the Union may have been less than honorable, it would be an important milestone in the history of African Americans. It would be hard to deny an African American man his citizenship after he had risked his life in battle for his country.

The use of African Americans was not enough to fill the Union ranks, however. In March 1863, Congress created the Northern draft, nearly a year after the Confederates began theirs. All men aged 20 to 45 were eligible. There were many ways to avoid service, however. Various health problems could exempt a man from serving. The rules also allowed a man to hire someone to fight in his place—usually poor young men or immigrants. Wealthy men could pay a fee of $300 and not have to fight this time. In the first draft call in July 1863, 207,000 men were drafted. But 87,000 paid the $300, and 74,000 found someone to take their place. In New York, the unfairness of the draft led to four days of riots. Whites attacked blacks. Homes and federal property were burned, and 105 people were killed before troops stopped the riots.

At last, in the spring of 1863, Lincoln again attempted to find himself a general who could bring the Union victories against the seemingly unbeatable General Lee. He chose General Joseph "Fighting Joe" Hooker. "May God have mercy on General Lee," said Hooker, "for I will have none."

Meanwhile, in March, Robert wrote home to Mary: "As for my health, I suppose I shall never be better." But within the next few weeks that would change. First Lee came down with a serious cold. On March 27, he wrote home again: "I have felt so unwell...as not to be able to go anywhere." On April 5: "I am suffering with a bad cold as I told you, and was threatened, the doctors thought, with some malady which must be dreadful if it resembles its name, but which I have forgot...I have not been so very sick, though have suffered a good deal of pain in my chest, back, and arms...The doctors have been very attentive and kind....They have been tapping me all over like an old steam boiler before condemning it."

The doctors called Lee's illness an "inflammation of the heart-sac." Historians now believe he had a mild heart attack. No one realized he had suffered permanent injury to his heart. On April 19, his letter to Mary included: "I am feeble and worthless and can do but little." In this weakened state he would soon face Fighting Joe Hooker.

The Union Army of the Potomac had 138,000 troops. Lee's Army of Northern Virginia had barely 60,000—he was outnumbered nearly two to one. The Union forces moved in from the west along the Rappahannock, heading for Fredericksburg. But the Confederates pounced on them sooner than expected. Hooker lost his nerve and pulled his troops back to a nearby town called Chancellorsville. Lee again took daring action. He divided his forces in two. Jackson would circle around Hooker's right flank for a surprise attack at the rear. Jeb Stuart's cavalry would cover them as they made their move.

Lee left many of the details of the maneuver to Jackson, whom he trusted completely. As they sat discussing last-minute strategies, Lee said, "General Jackson, what do you propose to make this movement with?"

"With my whole corps," Jackson answered.

Lee was surprised. "What will you leave me?"

"The divisions of Anderson and McLawd," Jackson answered.

That would leave Lee with only 14,000 men facing more than 50,000 Union troops. But the offensive move was the kind Lee liked: bold and well-planned.

"Well," he said, "go on."

He and Jackson had become an unusual team in battle. Jackson once said of Lee, "He is the only man I would follow blindfolded."

Of Jackson, Lee said only a few days later, "Such an executive officer the sun never shone on. I have but to show him my design, and I know that if it can be done, it will be done. No need for me to send or watch him. Straight as the needle to the pole he advanced to the execution of my purpose."

Lee's luck held on that day, May 2, 1863, and the plan worked beautifully. Jackson surprised the Union troops at the rear of Hooker's army as they were cooking their supper, and the dense woods filled with the sounds of battle. Lee attacked Hooker from the front to prevent him from sending reinforcements to his rear flank.

The battle went on into the dark night, and at some point Lee fell asleep on the ground. Around 2:30 A.M., Jackson's signal officer woke the sleeping general. The enemy had offered little resistance and had fled, he reported. The maneuver had been a resounding success. But there was bad news, too. As Jackson and a few of his officers had ridden forward in the dark night to scout the area, he had accidentally been shot by his own men, once in the right hand, twice in the left arm.

Lee was shaken, and he stopped the messenger with the words, "Ah, Captain, any victory is dearly bought which deprives us of the services of General Jackson, even for a short time!" At 3:00 A.M., he wrote to Stuart, "it is necessary that the glorious victory thus far achieved be prosecuted with the utmost vigor, and the enemy given no time to rally..." Stuart took over Jackson's troops, and the two wings of the Confederate army were reunited to send the confused Hooker and his troops fleeing.

It was another victory for Lee. But the cost of the Battle of Chancellorsville was high. There were 13,000 Confederate casualties, 17,000 for the Union. Even worse, during the night Jackson's left arm had to be amputated. When Lee received a note of congratulations from his loyal officer, and learned of his fate, he sent back the message: "Could I have directed events, I should have chosen for the good of the country to be disabled in your stead. I congratulate you upon the victory, which is due to your skill and energy."

Within days Jackson's condition grew worse; then he developed pneumonia. Lee refused to accept that he was in danger of losing his most trusted officer: "Give him my affectionate regards, and tell him to make haste and get well, and come back to me as soon as he can. He has lost his left arm; but I have lost my right arm."

Within days Jackson was dead. Neither Lee nor his army would ever recover from the loss.

GETTYSBURG

"Never mind, General, all this has been my
fault—it is I that have lost this fight…"

LEE SPEAKING TO GENERAL WILCOX
DURING THE BATTLE OF GETTYSBURG

Lee had little time to mourn the death of his chief lieutenant, for there was too much to do. His Army of Northern Virginia had continued to block Union advances on Richmond. He still seemed unbeatable. But the North was whittling away at the front in Mississippi, Tennessee, and North Carolina and tightening the blockade of Confederate seaports. Since November 1862, a man who had once fought side by side with Lee in Mexico—General Ulysses S. Grant—had been battering away at the Southern stronghold of Vicksburg, on the banks of the Mississippi River. The long struggle was taking place far from Virginia. But Lee knew a Grant victory would mean serious trouble. It would give Union forces full control of the Mississippi River, and split the Deep South in two.

Lee believed there was only one thing to do. He must once again attack the North on its own territory. Such a bold move would draw Grant's troops away from Vicksburg. When they reached there, they would be exhausted, and Lee would have the advantage. With the war now in its third year, perhaps a dramatic Confederate

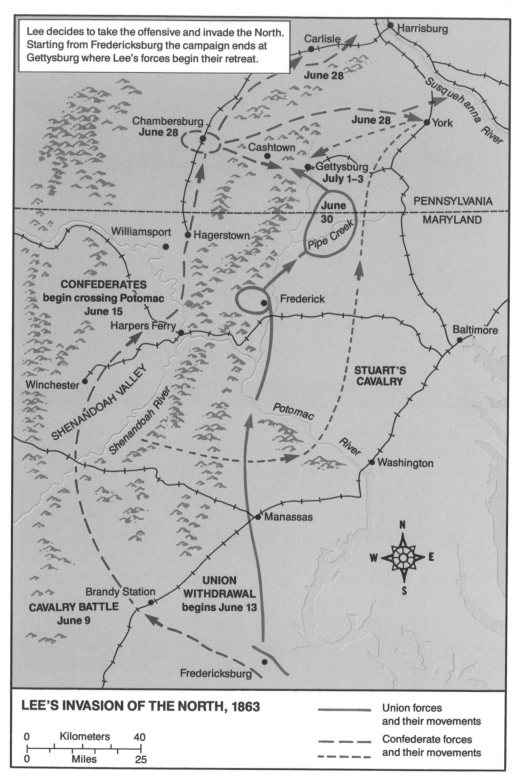

Lee decides to take the offensive and invade the North. Starting from Fredericksburg the campaign ends at Gettysburg where Lee's forces begin their retreat.

Harrisburg

Carlisle

June 28

Chambersburg
June 28

June 28   York

Cashtown

Gettysburg
July 1–3

June
30

PENNSYLVANIA

Pipe Creek

MARYLAND

Williamsport   Hagerstown

**CONFEDERATES
begin crossing Potomac
June 15**

Frederick

Harpers Ferry

Baltimore

**STUART'S
CAVALRY**

Winchester

SHENANDOAH VALLEY

Shenandoah River

Potomac

River

Washington

Manassas

N

W   E

S

Brandy Station

**UNION
WITHDRAWAL
begins June 13**

**CAVALRY BATTLE
June 9**

Fredericksburg

LEE'S INVASION OF THE NORTH, 1863

0   Kilometers   40

0   Miles   25

—————— Union forces
and their movements

— — — — Confederate forces
and their movements

success would convince Lincoln to settle for peace with Jefferson Davis and accept the South's independence.

First Lee reorganized his army into three divisions: one under General Longstreet, the second under General Richard S. Ewell, and the third under General A. P. Hill. Then he prepared to move his army into the rich, untouched farmlands of Pennsylvania and strike at that state's capital of Harrisburg. Coming after his success at Chancellorsville, he hoped it would be a major psychological blow to the war-weary North.

During the last hot days of June 1863, Lee led his army of 75,000 into Pennsylvania. Jeb Stuart, whom Lee had called the "eyes of the army," was sent off with his cavalry to shield the infantry's movement.

But this time, the dash and daring that had previously made Stuart so valuable to lee was Stuart's undoing. Only weeks before Stuart had been taken by surprise at Brandy Station by General Alfred Pleasonton in one of the largest cavalry battles of the war. Union casualties exceeded the Confederate losses, but Stuart suffered a great deal of public criticism over the incident. Now, while circling Union forces, Stuart spotted a chance to make up for the damage to his reputation with a daring capture of 125 supply wagons. As a result, Stuart was out of touch with the main army for a week. Without his "eyes," Lee continued blindly into Pennsylvania, with only rumors about the whereabouts of Union troops, led by General George G. Meade, to guide him.

Lee planned to gather his troops in a strong defensive position at a town called Cashtown. On June 30, a handful of advance troops wandered barefoot into the town of Gettysburg hoping to find shoes. Instead, they spotted Union soldiers.

The two armies had stumbled into each other unprepared, and the fight that neither side had planned turned into a bloody battle that none would ever forget.

On the morning of July 1, the fighting began north and west of town. A gunner recalled that "for seven or eight minutes ensued probably the most desperate fight ever waged between artillery and infantry at close range without a particle of cover on either

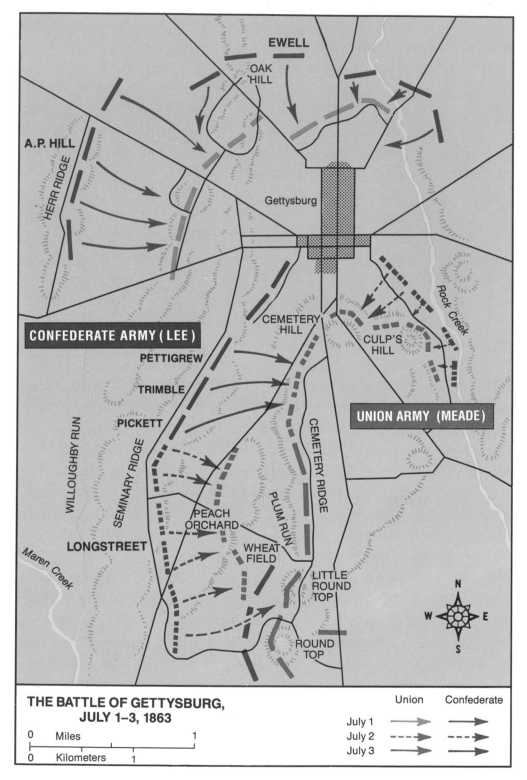

EWELL

OAK
HILL

A.P. HILL

HERR RIDGE

Gettysburg

CONFEDERATE ARMY (LEE)

CEMETERY
HILL

CULP'S
HILL

PETTIGREW

Rock Creek

TRIMBLE

UNION ARMY (MEADE)

PICKETT

CEMETERY RIDGE

WILLOUGHBY RUN

SEMINARY RIDGE

PLUM RUN

PEACH
ORCHARD

LONGSTREET

WHEAT
FIELD

Maren Creek

LITTLE
ROUND
TOP

ROUND
TOP

N
W E
S

**THE BATTLE OF GETTYSBURG,
JULY 1–3, 1863**

	Union	Confederate
July 1		
July 2		
July 3		

0   Miles   1

0   Kilometers   1

side... bullets hissing, humming and whistling everywhere; cannon roaring; all crash on crash and peal on peal, smoke, dust, splinters, blood, wreck and carnage [slaughter] indescribable." When Confederate reinforcements appeared, the outnumbered Union soldiers were soon sent running through the streets of Gettysburg and took up positions on Cemetery Hill, at the south end of town. Lee arrived and ordered Ewell to attack the fleeing Union troops, but the indecisive Ewell seemed paralyzed, unable to take action as Jackson would have done. Ewell's inaction cost Lee a chance to win a decisive battle at this point. By dawn, reinforcements had extended the Federal stronghold to Culp's Hill and south all along Seminary Ridge.

The Confederates took up position along Seminary Ridge to the west. On the morning of July 2, Lee pushed forward with an attack. He ordered Ewell to attack the north end of the Union line, and Longstreet to attack the south end. Ewell was to wait until he heard Longstreet's guns before beginning his attack. But Longstreet had his own ideas about how to continue the battle, and so failed to attack at dawn as ordered. Lee's method of fighting was to design an overall plan with his officers, and then trust them to carry out the details to the best of their ability. It was a style that worked well with an aggressive fighter such as Jackson, but was to fail miserably here with Longstreet and Ewell. As Lee's plans for an immediate strike became unraveled by the inaction and delay of his officers, reinforcements arrived for Union troops, who had time to become thoroughly entrenched in their positions. Still, Lee's all-out assault led to a bloody battle, and Union losses were heavy.

Lee faced the third day of battle with officers who no longer agreed that a direct attack was the best strategy. Lee claimed that the night before, he had once again ordered Longstreet to attack at dawn; the slow, cautious Longstreet wrote years later that Lee did not, and so Longstreet did not take action that morning. At 1:00 P.M., Confederate artillery began firing on the Union line, and Union cannon returned the fire for nearly two hours.

When the firing died down, Major General George Pickett led 15,000 brave soldiers up the hill in a direct assault on Cemetery

Ridge, where 6,000 Union soldiers awaited them. A Union soldier later described it as "an overwhelming restless tide of an ocean of armed men sweeping upon us!... on they move, as with one soul, in perfect order... over ridge and slope, through orchard and meadow and cornfield, magnificent, grim, irresistible."

But as the soldiers neared the stone walls and trees, Union fire suddenly rained down upon them. Rows of men fell to the ground, yet Pickett's men continued their hopeless charge. Some even passed over the stone walls, only to meet their death. Only a few survived to return to Confederate lines, defeated.

Such slaughter was one of the tragedies caused by Civil War officers using old ways of fighting in a new kind of war. Marching straight up to one's enemy was reasonable when soldiers carried what were called smoothbore muskets, which were not all that accurate and could strike a target only within about 100 yards or so. The advancing lines of soldiers had to get quite close to each other before they could hurt each other. Newer weapons—"rifled" muskets and cannons—had increased firing range. Now soldiers could begin killing each other within about a half-mile of one another. Hundreds of lives were lost—in movements such as Pickett's Charge—before these new lessons were learned.

An English reporter on the field wrote of Lee:

He was engaged in rallying and in encouraging the broken troops and was riding about a little in front of the wood, quite alone. His face, which is always placid and cheerful, did not show signs of the slightest disappointment, care, or annoyance; and he was addressing to every soldier he met a few words of encouragement, such as 'All this will come right in the end; we'll talk it over afterwards; but in the meantime all good men must rally. We want all good and true men just now.' He spoke to all the wounded men that passed him, and the slightly wounded he exhorted to 'bind up their hurts and take up a musket.' Very few failed to answer his appeal, and I saw many badly wounded men take off their hats and cheer him.

Late that evening, in the quiet aftermath of the battle, Lee rode out on Traveller to survey the condition of his army, to listen to the

cries of the wounded in the hot July night. About one o'clock, he slowly rode back through the moonlight to his headquarters. To the officers present, he said, "I never saw troops behave more magnificently than Pickett's division of Virginians did today in that grand charge upon the enemy. And if they had been supported as they were to have been—but, for some reason not yet fully explained to me, were not—we would have held the position and the day would have been ours. Victory might have led to an attack on Washington." He gazed into the dark night for a long moment, then cried out, "Too bad! *Too bad!* Oh! Too bad!"

Lee's threat to the North—his chance to strike a decisive blow—had been blocked at Gettysburg, the bloodiest single battle of the war for both sides. More than 50,000 men lost their lives in three days. Union casualties were 23,049; the Confederates had lost 28,063 men. A new wave of optimism would sweep the North, however. At last they had defeated the "indefeatable" Lee! Victory seemed possible again.

Southerners were shaken. Lee's army would never recover from the loss of men, officers, and morale. Historians would see the Battle of Gettysburg as the "high tide" of the Confederacy—the beginning of the end for the Southern cause.

For now, there was nothing left for Lee to do but retreat. Meade's army was too wounded to follow as Lee led his battered troops through the pouring rain south toward Virginia. So much had gone wrong, such good plans had been ruined by the lack of good officers. Lee wrote years later, "If I had had Stonewall Jackson with me...I should have won the battle of Gettysburg."

But he did not, and to the end he took all blame. When General Wilcox rode almost in tears to report what was happening, Lee said: "Never mind, General, all this has been my fault—it is I that have lost this fight."

The Beginning of the End

"It was a mere question of arithmetic to calculate
how long they could hold out."

ULYSSES S. GRANT, WRITING ABOUT LEE'S
ARMY OF NORTHERN VIRGINIA IN HIS *Memoirs*

Gettysburg was followed by more bad news. Lee learned that on July 4, General Ulysses S. Grant had won a complete victory at Vicksburg, Mississippi, bringing most of the western front into Union hands.

The public and the press were quick to criticize Lee for the failed campaign at Gettysburg, though his soldiers remained ever loyal. It was a major blow to Southern morale—and to Lee's. On August 8, 1863, Lee submitted his resignation. He wrote: "I therefore, in all sincerity, request Your Excellency to take measures to supply my place. I do this with the more earnestness because no one is more aware than myself of my inability for the duties of my position. I cannot even accomplish what I myself desire. How can I fulfill the expectation of others?" Within days President Davis sent his answer: "To ask me to substitute you by some one in my judgment more fit to command, or who would possess more of the confidence of the army, or of the reflecting men of the country, is to demand an impossibility..." The request was denied.

Lee continued in vain his campaigns to build up the army. The South had begun the war far inferior to the North in supplies and

By 1863, it seemed that Robert E. Lee was singlehandedly keeping the Confederacy from defeat.

manufacturing capabilities. Now, after three long years of war, the army was plagued by a shortage of everything: food, shoes, ammunition—and men.

On September 18–20, General Braxton Bragg won a Confederate victory at Chickamauga Creek, Georgia. Two months later, on November 25, the Union's General Grant defeated Bragg in Chattanooga, Tennessee. Slowly the Union was closing in on Lee's starving army.

That winter, Lee wrote letter after letter stressing the extreme lack of supplies, including one to the secretary of war: "A regular supply of provisions to the troops in this army is a matter of great importance. Short rations are having a bad effect upon the men, both morally and physically. Desertions to the enemy are becoming more frequent, and the men cannot continue healthy and vigorous if confined to this spare diet for any length of time. Unless there is a change, I fear the army cannot be kept together."

With his weakened, starving army, Lee had little hope of making further offensive attacks upon the North. His only chance was to build up the army for an enduring defense, one that would survive Union attacks until it simply wore down the enemy.

In the spring of 1864, Lincoln appointed Ulysses S. Grant commander in chief of the Union armies. Of all the Union generals, Grant alone seemed to have the guts and the endurance to accomplish Lincoln's goals. Grant had no shortage of supplies and had built up the Army of the Potomac to more than 130,000 men. Lee soon saw that Grant was coming for him. He wrote on April 6 to President Davis: "All the information I receive tends to show that the great effort of the enemy in this campaign will be made in Virginia... Reinforcements are certainly daily arriving to the Army of the Potomac... All the information that reaches me goes to strengthen the belief that General Grant is preparing to move against Richmond."

Less than a week later he wrote again: "Mr. President: My anxiety on the subject of provisions for the army is so great that I cannot refrain from expressing it to Your Excellency. I cannot see how we can operate with our present supplies. Any derangement [problem] in their arrival or disaster to the railroad would render it impossible for me to keep the army together, and might force a retreat into North Carolina. There is nothing to be had in this section for men or animals. We have rations for the troops to-day and to-morrow... Every exertion should be made to supply the depots at Richmond and at other points. All pleasure travel should cease, and everything be devoted to necessary wants."

On May 4, 1864, Grant led his army of nearly 130,000 well-equipped men south toward Richmond. Lee was delighted when Jeb Stuart and his cavalry brought word that Grant was taking the shortest route. That would lead his army right into the thick of the

Wilderness in northern Virginia, not far from where Lee had won the Battle of Chancellorsville the year before. Lee's men knew those thick woods and felt fighting there would give them an advantage, even though they were outnumbered. So Lee waited with his 60,000 troops until the Union soldiers were scattered in the woods.

On May 5, fierce fighting began in a strange, bloody battle in which soldiers fought unseen attackers. A Union private recalled the battle:

> No one could see the fight fifty feet from him. The roll and cackle of musketry was something terrible... The lines were very near each other, and from the dense underbrush and the tops of the trees came puffs of smoke, the 'oing' of the bullets and the yell of the enemy. It was a blind and bloody hunt to the death, in bewildering thickets, rather than a battle... The underbrush and briars scratched our faces, tore our clothing, and tripped out feet... Two, three and four times we rushed upon the enemy, but were met by a murderous fire and with heavy loss from concealed enemies.

The following morning, another delay by Longstreet left the Confederate line without reinforcements. Union soldiers attacked and drove back the broken Confederate lines. To their pleas for help, Lee sent word that they must hold the line as long as possible. Then suddenly, through the smoke of battle came about twenty Texans, members of Longstreet's troops. Lee raised himself in his stirrups and shouted above the sounds of battle: "Texans always move them!" With a whoop and a holler, the Texans charged into battle, and one soldier, tears running down his cheeks, exclaimed, "I would charge into hell itself for that old man!"

But when the men realized that Lee was heading with them into battle, they called out, "Go back, General Lee, go back!" Lee continued on, and the men shouted, "We won't go on unless you go back!" At last a sergeant took Traveller by the reins, and with reluctance Lee let the men go on without him.

The battle wore on all day. That night, fire broke out in the dry underbrush. The thick smoke made it hard to locate the wounded, and many who were unable to drag themselves away were lost in the fire.

Lee called the dashing J. E. B. Stuart "the eyes of the army."

In two days of fighting in the Battle of the Wilderness—May 5 and 6—Grant's army had suffered 14,000 casualties, while the South's were estimated at only 8,000. But unlike previous Union generals, Grant did not withdraw—he was in no way a quitter. And he would sacrifice his huge surplus of men to keep pounding away at the Southern resistance. On May 7, he moved his army away from the Wilderness, toward Spotsylvania Court House. Lee's troops met them there and built under fire a "mule shoe" fortification, an earthwork in the shape of a U. The fighting went on for almost two weeks, but it was at its worst on May 12 at a place that was to become known as the Bloody Angle. Here, in 17 hours of battle, more than 12,000 men fell in one of the bloodiest

days of the war. A Union private described it this way: "It was a
hand-to-hand conflict, resembling a mob in its character...for that
hour they were brutes, wild with passion and blood...The air was
filled with oaths, the sharp reports of rifles, thuds of clubbed
muskets, the swish of swords and sabers, groans, and
prayers...Federal and Confederate would roll on the ground in a
death struggle..."

Lee had halted Grant's attack, but like a dog who had finally
gotten his teeth into a bone, Grant was not going to let go. From
Spotsylvania he wrote Lincoln: "I propose to fight it out on this line
if it takes all summer."

By the end of May, Grant had lost 50,000 soldiers, and his
willingness to sacrifice his men brought him criticism from many
in the North, who called him "Butcher Grant." But Lincoln
believed that perhaps for once he had a general who stood a chance
of defeating the elusive Lee, and he would not recall him. "I cannot
spare this man. He fights," Lincoln said.

Meanwhile, Lee was hit with news of another loss. The Union's
General Philip Sheridan had ridden his cavalry around the Confederate Army to raid Richmond, but he had been stopped by Jeb

For more than 600,000 young men on both sides, this was how the war ended.

Stuart on May 11 in a battle at Yellow Tavern, seven miles north of Richmond. Unfortunately, Stuart took a bullet in the stomach and was not expected to live. Lee was visibly shaken upon reading the dispatch with that news. Then he folded up the paper and said, "General Stuart has been mortally wounded; a most valuable and able officer." Then, after a pause, he said, "He never brought me a piece of false information." When later that night he learned that Stuart had died, he hurried to his tent, and said to one of his officers, "I can scarcely think of him without weeping!" On May 16 he wrote his wife, "A more zealous, ardent, brave and devoted soldier than Stuart the Confederacy cannot have."

But the war went on. With 30,000 fresh troops, Grant continued his relentless battering of the Confederates. On June 3 at Cold Harbor, near the Chickahominy River, he attacked head-on in a massive assault that he hoped would break the Confederate line once and for all. He sacrificed more than 7,000 men in half an hour's battle, and the attack failed—Grant had failed to understand the defensive advantage of this new kind of trench warfare. Grant wrote in his *Memoirs*: "I have always regretted that the last assault at Cold Harbor was ever made." When another attack was ordered,

General Ulysses S. Grant (standing, with hat) was perhaps the only man in the Union army who could match Lee's brillance.

Union soldiers simply refused to move. The two armies faced each other from trenches for another 10 days.

Then Grant took a new direction. He sent cavalry out to cover his movements as he led his army of 100,000 around Richmond south of the James River. He was headed for Petersburg, a town 20 miles south of Richmond. He hoped to capture the railroads here. That would cut off the army and the capital from the rest of the South, and end completely their supplies of food. If he had succeeded, he might have ended the war right there. But Grant had entrusted the action to his own slow-moving General William F. Smith, who bungled the easy attack and gave Lee time to reach the city with reinforcements.

Many of the war's battles had been fought like gallant sporting matches, with two lines of soldiers bravely marching out to meet each other on a large field. But Petersburg was surrounded by 26 miles of well-built earthworks, and Lee immediately expanded them and settled his army in to wait. Grant's troops began to build their own set of trenches. It was not the first time trench warfare had been used in the Civil War. Here both sides took advantage of this new way of fighting. Mortar shells were launched to explode over the trenches, and sharpshooters kept up steady fire. Soldiers spent their time building bombproof shelters for protection and keeping the trenches dug out. Weeks of heat were followed by weeks of rain that left soldiers living in waist-deep water.

Many of Petersburg's citizens offered their homes to Lee, but he refused and set up his headquarters in a tent. When Lee's wife wrote to him expressing concern about his health, he wrote back, "But what care can a man give to himself in the time of war? It is from no desire for exposure or hazard that I live in a tent, but from necessity. I must be where I can, speedily, at all times, attend to the duties of my position, and be near or accessible to the officers with whom I have to act. I have been offered rooms in the houses of our citizens, but I could not turn the dwellings of my kind hosts into a barrack where officers, couriers, distressed women, etc., would be entering day and night..."

Sporadic but insistent fighting continued into the fall and winter. The casualties continued to pile up, but nothing was ever resolved.

As the tide of war turned, the South's supplies dwindled and Union supply posts filled with provisions.

Grant knew that direct assault would be useless here, so he simply hoped to wear Lee down with siege warfare—brutal, ceaseless bombardment. Lee had lost nearly a third of his officers. Grant wrote in his *Memoirs*: "It was a mere question of arithmetic to calculate how long they could hold out."

While good food and plenty of supplies poured in by train to the Union troops, Lee wrote in December to the secretary of war, "The struggle now is to keep the army fed and clothed. Only fifty men in some regiments have shoes, and bacon is only issued once in a few days." A Confederate officer wrote from the trenches, "It is hard to maintain one's patriotism on ashcake and water."

That fall, Major General William Tecumseh Sherman captured and then burned Atlanta, Georgia. Then, declaring "I can make...Georgia howl," he led his 60,000 men in a "march to the sea," destroying everything in their path—railroads, factories, farms, homes—anything that might be used to supply the Confederate army. It was a new kind of "total war" that struck soldier and civilian alike. It had no manners, no rules. Sherman wrote: "We cannot change the hearts of those people of the South, but we

WILLITS BRANCH LIBRARY

can make war so terrible...make them so sick of war that generations would pass away before they would again appeal to it." Before Christmas he would take Savannah. Sherman not only destroyed towns and farmlands. He also sowed the seeds of a great hatred that would grow among Southerners for generations to come.

That summer of 1864, as the war wore on, it had looked as if Lincoln might not be re-elected. Then came Sherman's bold successes in Atlanta and across Georgia. These successes helped Lincoln win re-election in November.

As the New Year dawned in 1865, it began to look as if the end of the war was near. General Philip Sheridan had taken over the Shenandoah Valley. Between him and Sherman, Confederate food sources were in non-Union hands. Sherman was beginning an unstoppable march north toward Virginia. Grant was tightening his grip on Lee. The Union blockade of Confederate ports was as tight as a noose.

Against this Union tide, only two Confederate armies were still bravely fighting in the field: Joseph E. Johnston's forces in North Carolina—and Robert E. Lee's Army of Northern Virginia.

Southerners dug in to defend Atlanta, but Sherman rolled over the defenses and torched the city.

SURRENDER

"There is nothing left for me to do but to go and see General Grant, and I would rather die a thousand deaths."

ROBERT E. LEE, ON FACING
SURRENDER TO ULYSSES S. GRANT

In January 1865, Fort Fisher fell to the Union, closing the South's last free port—Wilmington, North Carolina—and cutting off all supplies from the outside world. On February 3, a peace conference held in Hampton Roads, Virginia, between representatives from the North and South failed; Lincoln was now prepared to accept only unconditional surrender. Sherman was heading north.

Lee wrote the Confederate secretary of war: "You must not be surprised if calamity befalls us."

The Southern general also suffered personal tragedy. Union troops had occupied Arlington, his family's home, since the beginning of the war. The family's Washington heirlooms had been sent to the Patent Office for safekeeping. A federal tax had been placed on real estate, which had to be paid in person by the owners. A Lee cousin tried to pay the taxes, but the money was refused. On January 11, 1864, Arlington—which had been in Mary Custis Lee's family for generations—became the property of the United States government. Never again would Lee cross the threshold of the grand house where he had courted and married his wife—where all their children had been born. It was like losing his boyhood home

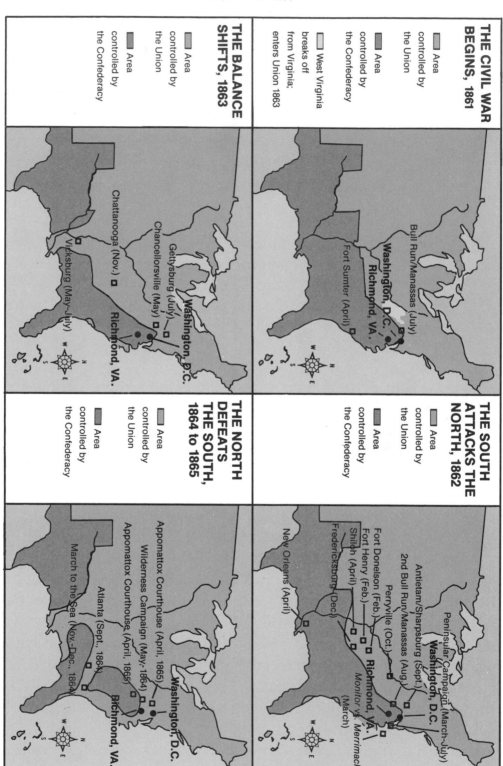

THE CIVIL WAR BEGINS, 1861

☐ Area controlled by the Union

■ Area controlled by the Confederacy

☐ West Virginia breaks off from Virginia; enters Union 1863

THE BALANCE SHIFTS, 1863

☐ Area controlled by the Union

■ Area controlled by the Confederacy

Chattanooga (Nov.)

Vicksburg (May–July)

Gettysburg (July)

Chancellorsville (May)

Washington, D.C.

Richmond, VA.

THE SOUTH ATTACKS THE NORTH, 1862

☐ Area controlled by the Union

■ Area controlled by the Confederacy

Bull Run/Manassas (July)

Fort Sumter (April)

Washington, D.C.

Richmond, VA.

THE NORTH DEFEATS THE SOUTH, 1864 to 1865

☐ Area controlled by the Union

■ Area controlled by the Confederacy

Appomattox Courthouse (April)

Wilderness Campaign (May–1864)

Appomattox Courthouse (April, 1865)

Atlanta (Sept., 1864)

March to the Sea (Nov.–Dec., 1864)

Washington, D.C.

Richmond, VA.

New Orleans (April)

Peninsular Campaign (March–July)

Antietam/Sharpsburg (Sept.)

2nd Bull Run/Manassas (Aug.)

Perryville (Oct.)

Fort Donelson (Feb.)

Fort Henry (Feb.)

Shiloh (April)

Fredericksburg (Dec.)

Washington, D.C.

Richmond, VA.

Monitor vs. Merrimack (March)

of Stratford Hall all over again. Later that year, on June 15, the Arlington grounds would become a national cemetery. In 1882, the Supreme Court would rule that the Arlington land belonged to Custis Lee, but by then it would be the burial site of thousands of soldiers. The government would pay Custis $150,000 for Arlington. One day far in the future, when the wounds of the broken Union had healed, Arlington would become the United States' most famous national cemetery and the site of the Tomb of the Unknown Soldier. For now, Lee suffered the loss with painful acceptance.

As Union armies whittled away at the Confederacy, many politicians, angered at Davis's apparent inaction, wanted to make Lee a military dictator. As a compromise with the Confederate Congress, Davis appointed Lee commander in chief of all Confederate forces. If he had been given such full command earlier in the war, it might have made a difference. Now, besieged behind the lines of Petersburg, with the situation hopeless on almost all other fronts, he could make little use of his new powers. He did recommend to Davis that all deserters be pardoned—so they could come back into the army as reinforcements. He also agreed to the proposal that slaves be allowed to enlist and given their freedom in return, as part of the "gradual and general emancipation" of slaves that Lee believed was now inevitable.

When asked in March what he thought of the military situation, Lee said that everything depended on food for the men and horses and on "the disposition and feelings of the people." He reported on shortages and thinning troops to Virginia's congressional representatives in Richmond. They assured him that the loyal people of Virginia would sacrifice whatever was asked of them. But they took no action.

One night after dinner, Lee paced in front of the fire while his son Custis sat reading the papers. Suddenly Lee said: "Well, Mr. Custis, I have been up to see the Congress and they do not seem to be able to do anything except to eat peanuts and chew tobacco, while my army is starving. I told them the condition the men were in, and that something must be done at once, but I can't get them to do anything, or they are unable to do anything."

SOUTHERN GLORY

As the war wound down, the hopes and dreams of the South slowly sputtered out. Behind the cries for independence from the Union lay a fierce pride in the Southern way of life. This way of life was tied to the traditional values of an agricultural society. In the ideal Southern world, gentlemen farmers managed their plantations, were kind to their slaves, and spoke and behaved with formality and civility. The proper Southern lady managed her household with aristocratic grace. Etiquette was admired above all things. Southerners fought for all of these things in the Civil War, believing that Northerners were out to destroy their way of life. Robert E. Lee—a man of brilliance, loyalty, and devotion—was in many respects the ideal Southern gentleman.

Robert E. Lee, the South's brightest hope, posed for the camera in 1865.

The Confederate capitol in Richmond represented the dreams of the South for an independent nation.

The destruction of Richmond following the Union army's invasion signaled an end to the dream of Southern glory.

The general paced some more, then said, "Mr. Custis, when this war began I was opposed to it, bitterly opposed to it, and I told these people that unless every man should do his whole duty, they would repent it; and now they will repent."

Lee's letters now suggested that he believed an end to the war was near. In a February 22 letter to the secretary of war, he wrote: "Grant, I think, is now preparing to draw out by his left with the intent of enveloping me. He may wait till his other columns approach nearing, or he may be preparing to anticipate my withdrawal. I cannot tell yet....Everything of value should be removed from Richmond. It is of the first importance to save all powder...."

On the same day he wrote to his wife: "After sending my note this morning, I received from the express office a bag of socks. You will have to send down your offerings as soon as you can, and bring your work to a close, for I think General Grant will move against us soon—within a week, if nothing prevents—and no man can tell what may be the result; but trusting to a merciful God, who does not always give the battle to the strong, I pray we may not be overwhelmed. I shall, however, endeavour to do my duty and fight to the last...."

On March 2, with Davis's permission, Lee wrote to Grant proposing an interview at which they would discuss a peace plan. Later that day he received painful news. Sheridan had defeated Confederate forces at Waynesboro, and would soon be heading north to join Grant's forces.

A few days later, Grant replied that he had no authority to negotiate a peace settlement. But by then Lee had already made plans with General John B. Gordon for one last attack on the Union lines. Before sunrise on March 25, Gordon made a bold strike in the center of the Union line and surprised the troops at Fort Stedman. But their early success was soon overturned when Union reserves counterattacked, and by eight o'clock that morning had killed, wounded, or taken prisoner more than 5,000 Confederate soldiers.

On the 26th, Lee wrote President Davis, "I fear now it will be impossible to prevent a junction between Grant and Sherman, nor do I deem it prudent that this army should maintain its position until the latter shall approach too near." He knew when they joined forces their troops would number 280,000 well-fed, well-armed men. Even with reinforcements from General Johnston, the Army of Northern Virginia would at most have 65,000 tattered, starving soldiers.

On March 29, fearing a Union attack on an important railroad line, Lee sent General Pickett to Five Forks to march on the enemy in the direction of Dinwiddie Courthouse. In an admirable battle, they fought off the Union cavalry. "Hold Five Forks at all hazards," Lee wrote to Pickett. "Protect road to Ford's Depot and prevent Union forces from striking the Southside Railroad." Another battle took place at Five Forks on April 1, but it was only afterward that Lee learned what had happened: His three generals, Thomas L. Rossner, Fitz Lee, and George Pickett, had not expected a quick follow-up attack, and had been surprised by Union troops while enjoying a shad bake. Lee lost more than 3,000 men and an important line of defense.

At dawn on April 2, General Grant began an all-out attack on Petersburg. Soon Lee sent word to President Davis, who received the message at 10:40 that morning in Richmond while attending the service at St. Paul's Church: "I advise that all preparation be made for leaving Richmond tonight. I will advise you later, according to the circumstances."

Lee was committed to holding Petersburg until nightfall. As he worked on the general order to evacuate the army that night, he received a telegram from Davis that indicated just how far removed from reality the president had become: He complained that leaving Richmond that night would "involve the loss of many valuables, both for the want of time to pack and of transportation."

In an unusual display of temper, Lee tore up the message and remarked, "I am sure I gave him sufficient notice." Then he sent a reply informing the president that it was absolutely necessary that he leave that night.

As darkness fell and Union fire died away for the night, Lee's army began its hasty retreat. Lee sat on Traveller and watched his soldiers cross the Appomattox River. Behind him, the sky was filled with the light of fires that had been set in Richmond to destroy the ammunition the departing troops could not carry with them. Meanwhile, Davis and his cabinet members were fleeing Richmond by train. By sunrise the capital would be in the hands of the Union army.

Lee's last hope was to meet up with what was left of Johnston's army. Now they headed for Amelia Courthouse, 40 miles away. Lee had arranged to have food sent there from Richmond by train to feed his hungry troops. But something went wrong. He found ammunition there, but no food. Lee was forced to spend an entire day scouring the surrounding area for food, but it was early spring and there was nothing to be had.

Union troops continued to harass the fleeing Confederate troops. On the evening of April 7, about half past nine, he received the following dispatch:

Headquarters Armies of the United States.
April 7, 1865—5 P.M.
General R. E. Lee,
Commanding C.S. Army:

General: The results of the last week must convince you of the hopelessness of further resistance on the part of the Army of Northern Virginia in this struggle. I feel that it is so, and regard it as my duty to shift from myself the responsibility of any further effusion of blood, by asking of you the surrender of that portion of the C.S. Army known as the Army of Northern Virginia.

Very respectfully, your obedient servant,

U. S. Grant
Lieutenant-General,
Commanding Armies of the United States

Wordlessly, Lee showed the message to Longstreet, who read it and said, "Not yet." Lee agreed and wrote Grant this answer:

7th Apl '65
Genl
I have recd your note of this date. Though not entertaining the opinion you express of the hopelessness of further resistance on the

part of the Army of N. Va.—I reciprocate [agree with] your desire to avoid useless effusion of blood, & therefore before considering your proposition, ask the terms you will offer on condition of its surrender.

> Very respy you obt. Servt
> R. E. Lee
> Genl
>
> Lt. Genl. U.S. Grant
> Commd Armies of the U. States

The next day Lee received word from Grant that he would insist only that Lee's officers and men be disarmed. He was ready to meet with Lee to settle the terms.

Lee held one last war council with his officers and asked for their advice. Instead of surrender, they chose to fight one last battle at Appomattox Courthouse. At 1:00 A.M. on April 9, Lee dressed with his best sword and a red silk sash. "I have probably to be General Grant's prisoner," he told an officer, "and thought I must make by best appearance." At five o'clock, Lee's meager army of 8,000 began one last attack. In only a few hours, it was all over. "Then there is nothing left for me to do," said Lee, "but to go and see General Grant, and I would rather die a thousand deaths."

"Oh, General," said one of his men, "what will history say of the surrender of the army in the field?"

Lee said simply, "I know they will say hard things of us. They will not understand how we were overwhelmed by numbers. But that is not the question, Colonel. The question is—is it right to surrender this army. If it is right, then I will take all the responsibility."

General E. P. Alexander suggested that instead of surrender, the men could take to the woods and continue to fight a guerrilla war.

Lee replied, "You and I as Christian men have no right to consider only how this will affect us. We must consider its effect on the country as a whole. Already it is demoralized by the four years of war. If I took your advice, the men would be without rations and under no control of officers. They would be compelled to rob and steal in order to live... We would bring on a state of affairs it would take the country years to recover from."

On April 9, 1865, Palm Sunday, Lee waited for half an hour in full dress uniform in the parlor of Major Wilmer McLean. It was a strange setting for the end of the war. For McLean had owned the farm where the first battle of Bull Run had been fought. After the second battle of Bull Run, he had sold his property and sought safety in the peaceful town of Appomattox Courthouse. Now the war was ending in his front yard.

At 1:30 P.M., Grant arrived, dressed in a field uniform splattered with mud. The two exchanged a few polite courtesies.

"I met you once before, General Lee," said Grant, "while we were serving in Mexico, when you came over from General Scott's headquarters to visit Garland's brigade, to which I then belonged. I have always remembered your appearance, and I think I should have recognized you anywhere."

"Yes," Lee said. "I know I met you on that occasion, and I have often thought of it and tried to recollect how you looked, but I have never been able to recall a single feature."

Grant then proceeded to chat about that war, until Lee politely brought him back to the current one.

"I suppose, General Grant, that the object of our present meeting is fully understood. I asked to see you to ascertain upon what terms you would receive the surrender of the army."

The two men then discussed the terms. Lee suggested that Grant write them down, and then sat patiently as the Union general lit his pipe and wrote out the text in pencil. Lee read halfway through it and noticed that a word had been inadvertently omitted.

"With your permission I will mark where it should be inserted."

"Certainly," Grant replied.

Lee completed his reading. All arms, artillery, and public property had to be surrendered, although all officers were allowed to keep their personal sidearms. All officers and men were to be allowed to return to their homes undisturbed.

"This will have a very happy effect on my army," Lee said. Then Grant said, "Unless you have some suggestions to make in regard to the form in which I have stated the terms, I will have a copy of the letter made in ink and sign it."

At this Lee hesitated, for the terms were generous, but then he said, "There is one thing I would like to mention. The cavalrymen and artillerists own their own horses in our army. Its organization in this respect differs from that of the United States. I would like to understand whether these men will be permitted to retain their horses."

"You will find that the terms as written do not allow this," said Grant. "Only the officers are allowed to take their private property."

Lee slowly looked over Grant's writing, and paused, but said only, "No, I see the terms do not allow it; that is clear."

Again Lee hesitated, and Grant was gracious enough not to force him to beg for his men. "Well, the subject is quite new to me. Of course, I did not know that any private soldiers owned their animals.... I take it that most of the men in the ranks are small farmers, and as the country has been so raided by the two armies, it is doubtful whether they will be able to put in a crop to carry themselves and their families through the next winter without the aid of the horses they are now riding.

"I will arrange it this way," said Grant. "I will not change the terms as now written, but I will instruct [my] officers . . . to let all the men who claim to own a horse or mule take the animals home with them to work their little farms."

"This will have the best possible effect upon the men," Lee said appreciatively. "It will be very gratifying and will do much toward conciliating our people."

While they waited for the ink copy to be drawn up, Grant offered to provide rations for Lee's remaining men, which the Southern general gratefully accepted.

By then a formal copy of Lee's acceptance of the terms was ready. It read:

Lieut-Gen. U. S. Grant
Commanding Armies of the United States.
General: I have received your letter of this date containing the terms of surrender of the Army of Northern Virginia as proposed by you.

As they are substantially the same as those expressed in your letter of the 8th instant, they are accepted. I will proceed to designate the proper officers to carry the stipulations into effect.
Very respectfully, your obedient servant,

Then, with no outward display of emotion, Lee put his signature to the surrender. It was 3:45 P.M., April 9, 1865. Although there were other Confederates who had yet to surrender, four long, cruel years of war were effectively over.

Lee soon rose and shook hands with Grant, then stepped out onto the porch. As he put on his hat, several Union officers jumped to their feet and gave him a formal salute, which Lee returned. At the top of the steps, he paused to pull on his gray gauntlets. He appeared to be lost in thought for a moment, quietly clapping his hands together as he looked out across the valley where his army sat waiting. Then, in a half-choked voice, he called out, "Orderly! Orderly!" At once Traveller was brought round, and Lee slowly mounted his faithful horse with a heavy sigh. Grant, heading for the gate, caught sight of the proud, handsome general and stopped. He removed his hat, and all who stood round the yard did the same.

Lee, sitting proud and erect in his saddle, raised his hat—then rode off to tell his faithful, worn-out soldiers of his surrender. And that all hope for Southern independence was gone.

As he rode into camp, the tattered, starving soldiers rushed to surround him.

"General," they cried, "are we surrendered?"

For once in his life, Lee could barely keep his composure. "Men," he managed to say, "we have fought the war together, and I have done the best I could for you." As tears filled his eyes, he could only mouth an inaudible good-bye before trying to move on.

Around him soldiers wept or cursed or stared into space, unable to believe that the end had come—that the Army of Northern Virginia had at long last surrendered.

The next morning, as Lee's final farewell address was being drawn up, General Grant had ridden over to see him but had been stopped at the picket lines. Lee was incensed by this rude behavior toward such a distinguished visitor and rode off on Traveller to meet him. The two men talked privately for more than half an hour. Grant recalled in his *Memoirs*: "I then suggested to General Lee that there was not a man in the Confederacy whose influence with the soldiery and the whole people was as great as his, and that if he would now advise the surrender of all the armies I had no doubt his advice would be followed with alacrity [speed]. But Lee said that he could not do that without consulting the President first. I knew there was no use to urge him to do anything against his ideas of what were right."

Lee returned to camp and signed several copies of General Orders No. 9, his farewell address. He gave no formal reading of it to the troops, only quietly distributed it among his officers.

Hd.qrs. Army of N. Va.
April 10, 1865

General Orders
No. 9

After four years of arduous [difficult] service marked by unsurpassed courage and fortitude, the Army of Northern Virginia has been compelled to yield to overwhelming numbers and resources.

I need not tell the brave survivors of so many hard fought battles, who have remained steadfast to the last, that I have consented to this result from no distrust of them; but feeling that valor and devotion could accomplish nothing that could compensate for the loss that must have attended the continuance of the contest, I determined to avoid the useless sacrifice of those whose past services have endeared them to their countrymen.

By the terms of the agreement, officers and men can return to their homes and remain until exchanged. You will take with you the satisfaction that proceeds from the consciousness of duty faithfully performed; and I earnestly pray that a Merciful God will extend to you His blessing and protection.

With an unceasing admiration of your constancy and devotion to your Country, and a grateful remembrance of your kind and generous consideration for myself, I bid you all an affectionate farewell.

(Sgd) R.E. Lee
Genl.

A SLOW REUNION

"I know you sorrow for us, but you must not be too much distressed. We must be resigned to necessity, & commit ourselves in adversity to the will of a merciful God as cheerfully as in prosperity. All is done for our good & our faith must continue unshaken."

LEE'S FIRST LETTER WRITTEN AFTER
THE WAR, TO HIS COUSIN MARKIE

ee did not attend the formal ceremony of surrender on the morning of April 12, 1865; he remained in camp until his men had returned from it.

A Union officer described the day:

Our earnest eyes scan the busy groups on the opposite slopes, breaking camp for the 1st time, taking down their little shelter tents and folding them carefully as precious things, then slowly forming the ranks as for unwelcoming duty. And now they move. The dusky swarms forge forward into gray columns of march. On they come, with the old swinging route step and swaying battleflags....

Gordon at the head of the column, riding with heavy spirit and downcast face, catches the sound of shifting arms, looks up, and taking the meaning, wheels superbly, making with himself and his horse one uplifted figure, with profound salutation as he drops the point of his sword to the boot toe; then facing to his own command, gives word for his successive brigades to pass us with the same position of the manual—honor answering honor. On our part not a sound of trumpet more, nor roll of drum; not a cheer, nor word nor whisper of vain-glorying, but an awed stillness rather, and breath-holding, as if it were the passing of the dead.

Then, with a few of his officers, Lee rode for home. Word of his coming traveled faster than he did, and along the way people ran out to see him. Women brought out food. On the night of April 14, he stopped to spend the night at his brother's farm in Powhatan County. The house was crowded, and Lee insisted on spending the night in his old tent pitched on the lawn.

On April 15, Lee rode through the rain into the ruins of Richmond. The skyline along the James River was a jagged edge of burned-out buildings. Much of the once-proud capital of the Confederacy was now a cemetery of destroyed homes, factories, warehouses, and shops. Above the capitol building waved the symbol of the occupied city's defeat: the Stars and Stripes of the Union flag.

Despite the rain, Southerners and Northerners alike turned out into the rubble-filled streets to stare in awe at him or to greet him with cheers and tears.

At last Lee came to 707 East Franklin Street, the home his wife had set up during the war. He bowed to the crowd, then went inside and took off his sword for the last time.

Sometime that day, Lee must have learned along with the rest of Richmond the shocking news from Washington. The night before, President Lincoln had been assassinated by an actor named John Wilkes Booth while attending a play at Ford's Theatre. He had died at 7:22 that very morning. Lee wrote later: "It is a crime previously unknown to this country, and one that must be deprecated by every American." Lincoln had been ready to work out a positive, sympathetic reunion with white Southerners. Now the South's future was unclear.

Richmond was immediately put under tough restrictions. Though the war had all but ended with Lee's surrender, the Confederate government had not formally surrendered. Johnston was still just outside of Raleigh, North Carolina, with uncaptured troops. President Davis, still out of touch with reality, was fleeing south with his cabinet, hoping to reach Mississippi and continue the fight. At last, on April 26, Johnston surrendered to Sherman. Davis was captured. And with a new president, Andrew Johnson, in the White House, the country began the slow, painful process of returning the war-torn states to the Union.

President Johnson and Congress now began the long process of knitting North and South back together. It was a difficult problem, and there was a great deal of disagreement among Northerners on how Southerners should be treated. Should there be a universal pardon? Or should they be punished as traitors?

Then a district court judge called for Lee and other Confederates to be tried for treason. On July 13, Lee wrote a formal request for pardon to President Andrew Johnson and forwarded it to Grant, asking if he would add his recommendation. Grant passed the request on to the president with his endorsement.

In asking for amnesty, Lee became a symbol for many Southerners, who now felt they could honorably accept Johnson's pardon. However, though Lee was never brought to trial, he was never formally pardoned until long after his death.

Lee accepted the defeat graciously and urged his fellow Southerners to quickly devote themselves to the rebuilding of the South and the Union. "I believe it to be the duty of every one to unite in the restoration of the country, and the establishment of peace and harmony," he wrote that September.

With the war over, Lee hoped to move to a small house in the country and find some means of earning a living. He even planned to write a book about his campaigns.

Then, in August, Lee was visited by John W. Brockenbrough, the rector of Washington College in Lexington, Virginia. He told Lee that the modest institution had voted to elect him president and wondered if he would consider accepting the job, at a salary of $1,500 a year, plus a house and garden and one-fifth of the students' tuition fees, which had just been increased to $75.

Lee was quite surprised by the offer. Lee wrote some days later expressing his concern. He wondered whether he had the strength to handle the job. He worried that the fact that he had not yet been granted amnesty might subject the school to "a feeling of hostility." But then he added, "Should you, however, take a different view, and think that my services in the position... will be advantageous to the College and Country, I will yield to your judgment and accept it; otherwise, I must most respectfully decline the office."

The trustees of Washington College did think otherwise, and they were thrilled to have Lee accept their invitation. The college had been founded in 1749 as Augusta College, but was later renamed after Lee's hero, George Washington, who had donated 100 shares of James River Company stock to the school in 1796. The war had done its damage to this small college, as well as to others throughout the South. There were only a handful of teachers, and not many more students, for few young Southern men had any money to spend on education. Loans were needed to repair the buildings and operate the school.

Despite these problems, once Lee was inaugurated in his new position on October 2, he devoted himself to rebuilding the college as if it were the top university in the nation. Within a year the school had 14 teachers and 146 students—and there were 400 by the fall of 1867, some even from Northern states.

In his five years as an administrator, Lee raised funds, expanded and improved the curriculum to include elective courses, and made Washington College one of the most admired institutions of higher education in the South. He was the first to include courses in commerce and journalism, and he expanded the curriculum to include practical courses that would help students get jobs in the tough world that waited for them. He demanded that his students work hard, but rather than use harsh discipline, he expected them to master themselves willingly through an honor system. When a new student once asked him for the college's rule book, Lee replied, "We have no printed rules. We have but one rule here, and that is that every student must be a gentleman." Eventually, Washington College would be renamed Washington and Lee University, in Lee's honor.

Lee also spent much of his time personally answering the hundreds of letters that poured in from around the country, many from former soldiers or comrades in the war. But wherever he went, in word and deed, he encouraged his countrymen to turn their eyes to the future; to be done with the destruction of the four

Lee in retirement, posed on his trusted horse Traveler in 1868.

years of war and to get on with growing and rebuilding; to replace bitterness with humble acceptance. When one woman spoke bitterly of the war, Lee said, "Madam, don't bring up your sons to detest the United States Government. Recollect that we form one country now. Abandon all these local animosities and make your sons Americans."

By 1869, Lee's health began to fail, and he suffered again from what doctors termed "inflammation of the heart-sac." In March 1870, at age 63, he took a leave from his post at Washington College. With his daughter Agnes he toured the South, visiting old friends, and everywhere he went he was greeted with respect, awe, admiration...and love. When he visited the once-familiar grounds of Shirley Plantation, where his mother had been raised, one of the residents recorded the general reaction of the household: "We regarded him with the greatest veneration... We had heard of God, but here was General Lee!"

In September Lee returned to his duties at Washington College. On September 27, a cold, windy, rainy day, Lee put on his long military cape from the war and went to a meeting at four o'clock in Grace Church. When he came home drenched, he went into the dining room to join his family, who had been waiting tea for him. Lee was never one to be late, so Mrs. Lee said, "You have kept us waiting a long time. Where have you been?"

Lee did not answer, but stood by his chair as if to say grace. Then he sat down in his chair with a look of utter resignation. His family could tell by looking at him that something was wrong. They immediately sent for the doctor. Lee had suffered a stroke. For two weeks he lingered, fading in and out of consciousness, speaking commands on battlefields revisited in dreams. On the morning of October 12, a little after nine o'clock, those who waited at his bedside heard him say with finality, "Strike the tent." And then he was gone.

EPILOGUE

Robert E. Lee was a reluctant hero in one of the most devastating dramas in American history—the American Civil War.

He was a soldier who loved peace. He did not believe in slavery or in the destruction of the Union. Yet he chose to lead the army of the new Confederate nation, whose people broke from the Union over States' right to act on those issues in their own way.

It was by far the most difficult choice in Lee's life. Did his first loyalty belong to the young nation of his ancestors—the nation created by his hero, George Washington? Or did it belong to his home state? How could a man of honor make such a choice? Indeed, it was one he had hoped and prayed he would not have to make.

In the end, his deepest loyalty was rooted in the Virginia soil. "I have not been able to make up my mind to raise my hand against my relatives, my children, my home..." he wrote to his sister Anne, "and save in defense of my native State...I hope I may never be called upon to draw my sword."

But draw his sword he must. In accepting command of the Army of Northern Virginia, he became one of the most admired generals of all time. His only fault, most historians agree, was that he was too polite a commander—that he trusted weaker men to act with the same honor and faith that governed his own actions. Against great odds, he used intelligence and strategy to defeat nearly every general President Abraham Lincoln could send against him: Pope, McClellan, Burnside, Hooker. With great persistence and military skill, he even held out against the relentless battering of General Ulysses S. Grant, the general who would at last draw his surrender. Even then, he gave up only because he could no longer bear to pursue a hopeless cause that could only bring more suffering to the Southern people whom he loved.

Grant, the only man to best the Southern general, admired Lee's dignity in defeat. When Union troops began to whoop and holler with joy over Lee's surrender, Grant quickly put an end to the celebration. In his memoirs Grant wrote, "The Confederates were now our prisoners, and we did not want to exult over their downfall."

After the war Lee was a model of gracious defeat—and that attitude would win him admirers among friends and foes alike. He did not spend his last years in bitter regret. Instead, as head of Washington College, he taught young Southern men the skills they needed to build a new life and a new future. He appealed to the defeated people of the South to put aside their hatred and bitterness and join him in rebuilding the United States of America.

Lee was an aristocrat without money or land. Yet his manners and code of ethics far outshone those of the people around him. His deep religious faith led him to accept with good heart the disappointment and hardships of his life: the fallen fortunes of his father, Light-Horse Harry Lee; the responsibilities of caring for an invalid mother—and later an invalid wife; the tardy promotions of his military career; the loss of Stratford Hall, and later Arlington; and finally, defeat in the Civil War.

TIMETABLE OF EVENTS IN THE LIFE OF
ROBERT E. LEE

Jan. 19, 1807	Born in Northern Virginia
1829	Graduates from West Point as Brevet Second Lieutenant in the Corps of Engineers
1831	Marries Mary Lee Fitzhigh Custis
1834	Appointed assistant to the Chief of Engineers in the War Department
1837	Helps reroute the Mississippi
1836	Promoted to first lieutenant
1838	Promoted to captain
1846–52	Serves in Mexican War
1852	Appointed superintendent of West Point
1859	Puts down John Brown's raid on Harpers Ferry, Virginia
1860	Assigned command of the Department of Texas
1861	Resigns from the United States Army
1862	Appointed commander of the Army of Northern Virginia Wins Second Manassas, or Second Battle of Bull Run Defeated during invasion of the North Wins battle at Fredericksburg, Virginia
1863	Wins battle at Chancellorsville, Virginia Defeated during second invasion of the North
1865	Surrenders to Grant at Appomattox Courthouse
Oct. 12, 1870	Dies in Lexington, Virginia

Suggested Reading

*Bains, Rae. *Robert E. Lee, Brave Leader*. Mahwah, N.J.: Troll, 1985.

Carter, Hodding. *Robert E. Lee and the Road of Honor*. New York: Random House, 1955.

*Commager, Henry Steele and Lynd Ward. *America's Robert E. Lee*. Boston: Houghton Mifflin, 1951.

Daniels, Jonathan. *Robert E. Lee*. Boston: Houghton Mifflin, 1960.

Graves, Charles P. *Robert E. Lee, Hero of the South*. Champaign, Ill.: Garrard, 1964.

*Monsell, Helen A. *Robert E. Lee: Young Confederate*. New York: Macmillan, 1983.

Weidhorn, Manfred. *Robert E. Lee*. New York: Atheneum, 1988.

*Readers of *Robert E. Lee and the Rise of the South* will find these books particularly readable.

SELECTED SOURCES

ROBERT E. LEE

Davis, Burke. *Gray Fox*. New York: Rinehart, 1956.

Freeman, Douglas Southall. *Lee*. An abridgement in one volume by Richard Harwell of the four-volume *R. E. Lee*. New York: Charles Scribner's Sons, 1961.

Freeman, Douglas Southall. *R. E. Lee*. 4 vols. New York: Charles Scribner's Sons, 1934.

Horn, Stanley F. *The Robert E. Lee Reader*. New York: Grosset & Dunlap, 1949.

Lee, R.E. Jr. *Recollections and Letters of General Robert E. Lee*. New York: Doubleday, Page, 1904.

Van Doren Stern, Philip. *Robert E. Lee, The Man and the Soldier. A Pictorial Biography*. New York: McGraw Hill, 1963

THE CIVIL WAR

Catton, Bruce. *The American Heritage Picture History of the Civil War*. New York: American Heritage/Bonanza Books, 1960 (1982 edition).

Catton, Bruce. *The Civil War*. New York: American Heritage Press, 1960, 1971.

Catton, Bruce. *Reflections on the Civil War*. New York: Berkley Books, 1982.

Davis, Burke. *The Civil War, Strange and Fascinating Facts*. New York: Fairfax Press, 1982.

McPherson, James M. *Battle Cry of Freedom*. New York: Random House, Ballantine Books, 1989.

Index

Cathy East Dubowski has written more than 25 books for children, including *Clara Barton: Healing the Wounds* and *Andrew Johnson: Rebuilding the Union*, also in this series, and the Random House "Step into Reading" books *Pretty Good Magic* and *Cave Boy*, which her husband Mark coauthored and illustrated. She currently works as a writer and editor in Chapel Hill, North Carolina, where she lives with her husband and five-year-old daughter, Lauren.

PICTURE CREDITS

Library of Congress: 17, 34, 43, 59, 69, 78, 79, 98, 101, 102, 103, 105, 106, 110, 111, 124. B&O Railroad Museum: 51.

Cover: Culver Pictures: portrait, map. The Granger Collection: Lee and his generals.